TECHNICAL
REPORT

Air Force Officer Specialty Structure

Reviewing the Fundamentals

Raymond E. Conley, Albert A. Robbert

Prepared for the United States Air Force

Approved for public release; distribution unlimited

RAND PROJECT AIR FORCE

The research described in this report was sponsored by the United States Air Force under Contract FA7014-06-C-0001. Further information may be obtained from the Strategic Planning Division, Directorate of Plans, Hq USAF.

Library of Congress Cataloging-in-Publication Data

Conley, Raymond E.
Air Force officer specialty structure : reviewing the fundamentals / Raymond E. Conley, Albert A. Robbert.
p. cm.
Includes bibliographical references.
ISBN 978-0-8330-4619-2 (pbk. : alk. paper)
1. United States. Air Force—Officers. 2. United States. Air Force—Occupational specialties.
3. United States. Air Force—Job descriptions. 4. United States. Air Force—Personnel management.
I. Robbert, Albert A., 1944– II. Title.

UG793.C66 2009
358.4'13320973—dc22

2009023866

Published 2009 by the RAND Corporation
1776 Main Street, P.O. Box 2138, Santa Monica, CA 90407-2138
1200 South Hayes Street, Arlington, VA 22202-5050
4570 Fifth Avenue, Suite 600, Pittsburgh, PA 15213-2665
RAND URL: http://www.rand.org/
To order RAND documents or to obtain additional information, contact
Distribution Services: Telephone: (310) 451-7002;
Fax: (310) 451-6915; Email: order@rand.org

Preface

U.S. Air Force specialty codes, similar to Army and Marine Corps military occupational specialties and Navy officer designators and enlisted ratings, establish personnel-classification boundaries according to the work performed and the required skills, education, and training. The specialties combine duties and tasks into cohesive job clusters that may be matched to people possessing the essential aptitudes, attributes, and qualifications. Given the Air Force's evolving missions, changing nature of work, and changing workforce, several senior Air Force leaders have asked whether the existing specialty codes still provide the appropriate clustering of specialties.

This technical report examines the current officer-classification structure while seeking to determine whether more fundamental changes are needed. It provides a brief primer on the specialty-classification system, encapsulates major changes that are in progress and planned, and offers additional changes based on interviews and comparative analyses. Although the research focused primarily on the officer structure, many of the observations have correlates in the enlisted-specialty structure.

The research was sponsored by the Deputy Chief of Staff, Manpower, Personnel, and Services, Headquarters United States Air Force (USAF) (AF/A1). The work was conducted within the Manpower, Personnel, and Training program of RAND Project AIR FORCE for a fiscal year (FY) 2007 study, "USAF Specialty Code Restructuring." This report should interest Air Force human resource managers and planners, as well as those in the other military services.

RAND Project AIR FORCE

RAND Project AIR FORCE (PAF), a division of the RAND Corporation, is the U.S. Air Force's federally funded research and development center for studies and analyses. PAF provides the Air Force with independent analyses of policy alternatives affecting the development, employment, combat readiness, and support of current and future aerospace forces. Research is conducted in four programs: Force Modernization and Employment; Manpower, Personnel, and Training; Resource Management; and Strategy and Doctrine.

Additional information about PAF is available on our Web site:
http://www.rand.org/paf/

Contents

Figures and Tables

Figures

Tables

Summary

Since its inception over 50 years ago, the Air Force specialty-classification structure has had only one major overhaul—in 1993. Yet, the Air Force has changed dramatically. It is smaller. Its people are more educated and experienced. Its missions have continued to evolve. Given the evolving missions, changing workforce, and changing nature of work, several senior Air Force leaders are asking whether the existing specialty codes provide the correct blend or combination (*natural clusters*) of specialties.

Several representatives from RAND Project AIR FORCE were asked to serve as members of an Air Force Specialty Code (AFSC) Reengineering Working Group assembled by the Air Force to assess the clustering of specialty codes. In addition, PAF was asked to determine whether other classification changes might be warranted. This technical report presents those results by examining the current officer-classification structure while seeking to determine whether more fundamental changes are needed.

The research began with an analysis of historical major changes in the classification structure. Later, the RAND team conducted interviews with Air Staff, major command (MAJCOM), and Air Force Personnel Center (AFPC) specialty-classification personnel and users of the system, such as functional managers, assignment managers, and occupation analysis specialists. Additional information was obtained during briefings given by functional managers to the AFSC Reengineering Working Group. Historical documents, as well manpower and personnel data obtained primarily from Air Force manpower and personnel databases, were used to verify information received during interviews and briefings and to identify potential issues and extant patterns for comparative analyses.

The research offers four conclusions and seven recommendations. The conclusions are as follows:

- The framework for officer specialty classification is fundamentally sound: It helps match military jobs and personnel for Air Force purposes and facilitates a common occupational language between information systems. Given its current use and operating environment, major modifications to the structure are not required (pp. 10–12, 23–25).
- Specialty-classification components need continuous maintenance (i.e., adjustments for changes in characteristics of the work and/or workers) and periodic upgrades to capitalize on best practices and improved technology (pp. 13–17).
- Major changes are occurring in the Air Force, Department of Defense (DoD), the nature of work, and the nature of modern warfare. They will lead to significant changes in the specialty-classification structure (pp. 14–21, 28–38).
- Observations made about the officer structure may have relevant correlates in the enlisted specialty-classification structure (pp. 25–26).

The recommendations are as follows:

- Expand the continuous process improvement initiatives, Air Force Smart Operations 21 (AFSO21), to include reducing the overall cycle time for specialty-classification changes.
- Revise the current classification tenets—many of which are administrative guidelines—to reflect best practices from human capital management.
- Add a column to unit manpower documents (UMDs) for secondary specialties. Let the increased visibility and normal refinement processes improve the accuracy of those requirements.
- Use the migration to the Defense Integrated Military Human Resources System (DIMHRS) as an opportunity to (1) eliminate data elements that add little value or duplicate information derived elsewhere and (2) add variants for codes that specify broad groups of specialties (jobs for which specific backgrounds are not required—"any officer" codes).
- Increase discipline in the officer special-experience identifier (SEI) system by establishing relationships and edits[1] between the SEI codes and applicable AFSCs.
- Increase the granularity of officer Intelligence specialties by using suffixes if it is not possible to put discipline in the SEI system.
- Initiate research to assess the potential effects of the changing nature of work and warfare on the specialty-classification structure.

---

[1] *Edits* reflect the relationship between the AFSC and the SEI code.

Acknowledgments

Many people provided valuable assistance and support throughout this research effort. We owe special thanks to Maj Gen K. C. McClain for initiating the study and to John Park (AF/A1PF) and Lt Col Suzanne Wheeler (AF/A1PF) for being active sponsors. Also, we give thanks to the many people at the Air Force Personnel Center who opened their files and shared decades of experience with us. In particular, we thank Barry Craigen and Leon Anderson of the Classification Development Branch. We thank the members of the various assignment and development teams who shared their thoughts and experiences. We thank Robert Whitley for sharing his knowledge about the Defense Integrated Military Human Resources System.

At the Air Force Occupational Measurement Squadron, we extend thanks to Lt Col James Wisnowski and Shirlene LeBleu for sharing their database and insights about job content and specialty analyses. At the Air Force Manpower Agency, we thank Col Kenneth Keskel and Ruby Manen for sharing their insights about the implications of specialty changes for the manpower-requirements determination processes. Also, we thank Maj Ernest Wearren (AF/A1MZ) and Gary Stockinger (AF/A1MX) for sharing their knowledge of the Manpower Programming Execution System and its interface with other personnel and financial management data systems. We thank Greg Parton (AF/A1MR) and William Booth (AF/A1M) for helping us explore ways the Air Force might think "out-of-the-box" about specialty requirements.

We are also grateful to the many career-field managers who provided briefings to the Air Force Specialty Code (AFSC) Reengineering Working Group. We want to give special thanks also to those who participated in interviews, including CMSgt Bruce Collet (SAF/XCID) and CMSgt Timothy Tate (AF/A4RF).

Abbreviations

ACC	Air Combat Command
ACD	activity code designator (U.S. Navy)
AETC	Air Education and Training Command
AFB	Air Force Base
AFCFM	Air Force Career Field Manager
AFECD	Air Force Enlisted Classification Directory
AFI	Air Force Instruction
AFOCD	Air Force Officer Classification Directory
AFOMS	Air Force Occupational Measurement Squadron
AFPC	Air Force Personnel Center
AFS	Air Force specialty
AFSC	Air Force specialty code
AFSO21	Air Force Smart Operations 21
AIA	Air Intelligence Agency
AMC	Air Mobility Command
AOC	area of concentration (U.S. Army)
AQD	additional qualification designator
ASI	additional skill identifiers
AWACS	Airborne Warning and Control System
C2	command and control
CFETP	Career Field Education and Training Plan
CHCO	Chief Human Capital Officer
CoCOM	combatant command
CSAF	Chief of Staff of the Air Force
DA	Department of the Army
DAF	Department of the Air Force
DIA	Defense Intelligence Agency

DIMHRS	Defense Integrated Military Human Resources System
DMDC	Defense Management Data Center
DN	Department of the Navy
DoD	Department of Defense
DRU	Direct Reporting Units
DTRA	Defense Threat Reduction Agency
EAF	expeditionary aerospace forces
EOD	explosive ordnance disposal
EW	electronic warfare
FA	functional area
FAC	forward air control
FAQ	frequently asked question
FCCME	Facilities, Contract/Construction Management Engineer
FOA	Field Operating Agencies
FY	fiscal year
JCS	Joint Chiefs of Staff
KSA	knowledge, skills, and abilities
LCOM	Logistics Composite Model
LDO	limited duty officer
MAGTF	Marine Air-Ground Task Force
MAJCOM	major command
MCTFS	Marine Corps Total Force System
MOS	military occupational specialty
MOSC	military occupational specialty code
MPES	Manpower Programming and Execution System (U.S. Air Force)
NAF	Numbered Air Force
NCO	noncommissioned officer
NEC	Navy Enlisted Classification
NFO	Naval Flight Officers (U.S. Navy)
NRL	nonrated line
OPMS	Officer Personnel Management System (U.S. Army)
OSI	Office of Special Investigations
OTS	Officer Training School

PDS	personnel data system
PME	professional military education
QDR	Quadrennial Defense Review
RECCE	reconnaissance
RI	reporting identifier
RL	rated line
SD	special duty
SDI	special-duty identifier
SDO	special-duty officer
SEAL	Sea Air Land special force
SecAF	Secretary of the Air Force
SEI	special-experience identifier
SI	skill identifier
SME	subject-matter expert
SOF	Special Operations Forces
SPEC	space professional experience code
SSP	subspecialty (Navy)
T&E	AF Operational Test and Evaluation
Tech App	AF Technical Application Center
TPR	trained personnel requirement
UAV	unmanned aerial vehicle
UDT	Underwater Demolition Team (U.S. Navy)
UMD	unit manpower document
URL	Unrestricted Line (U.S. Navy)
USAF	U.S. Air Force
USAFA	U.S. Air Force Academy
USMC	United States Marine Corps

CHAPTER ONE

Introduction

Air Force specialty code (AFSC) classifications have continued in their present form, with minor changes, since the mid-1990s.[1] Yet, the Air Force itself has changed dramatically: *It is smaller.* In 1995, the Air Force had more that 400,000 active duty members; in 2007, it had less than 335,000. *Its people are more educated and experienced*: In 1995, about 50 percent of the enlisted force had at least some college education; by 2007, the percentage surpassed 70. The younger officers and enlisted personnel have grown up with computers, video games, portable communications devices, and the Internet—affording them more virtual and real experiences than past generations. *Its missions continue to evolve*: The late 1990s witnessed growth in the number of contingencies requiring deployed forces, bringing about the maturation of the expeditionary aerospace forces (EAF) concept. In 2005, citing the realities and importance of cyber operations, the Air Force expanded its mission statement to encompass air, space, and cyberspace.[2] Given the evolving missions, changing workforce, and changing nature of work, several senior Air Force leaders are asking whether the existing specialty codes provide the correct blend, or combination (natural clusters), of specialties.[3]

Purpose of This Report

This report addresses the current officer-classification structure, seeking to determine whether more fundamental changes are needed. Several representatives from RAND Project AIR FORCE (PAF) were asked to serve as members of an Air Force Specialty Code (AFSC) Re-engineering Working Group tasked by the Air Force to assess the clustering of specialty codes.[4] In addition to serving on the working group, PAF was asked to determine whether other changes might be warranted.[5] This report focuses primarily on the officer-specialty structure; however, for amplification or clarification, it occasionally refers to the enlisted structure.

[1] The last complete revision of the Air Force specialty-classification structure was implemented in October 1993. It was a Chief of Staff of the Air Force (CSAF)-directed initiative that created fundamental changes in most of the specialty codes.

[2] The Secretary of the Air Force (SecAF) and CSAF announced the change in December 2005.

[3] In 2006, CSAF tasked the director of Manpower and Personnel (AF/A1) to lead an AFSC Reengineering Working Group. As another example, the logistics community initiated a separate review of several specialties, as did the communication and computer community.

[4] The members selected from RAND had extensive backgrounds in human capital management and had been involved in several research efforts spanning most elements of the Air Force's current system.

[5] The working group's findings on the combining of specialties were briefed by the AF/A1 to senior leaders in October 2007.

Research Methodology

The research began with a longitudinal analysis of major changes in the classification structure. Later, the research team conducted 18 interviews with Air Staff, major command (MAJCOM), and Air Force Personnel Center (AFPC) specialty classification personnel and users of the structure and associated systems, such as functional managers, assignment managers, and occupation analysis specialists—suppliers and users of specialty data. These interviews were designed to identify issues and their implications.[6] A copy of the interview protocol is provided in Appendix A. Additional information was obtained during briefings given by functional managers to the AFSC reengineering working group. To verify information received during interviews and briefings and to clarify potential issues and extant patterns for comparative analyses, we referred to historical documents and to manpower and personnel data.

Organization of the Report

The report has five sections and two appendixes. Chapter Two serves as a primer on the classification system, reviewing fundamental classification concepts and tenets, the coding schema, and major uses. Chapter Three reviews prominent past changes, as well as major changes that are in progress or planned. Chapter Four looks beyond these changes by offering others based on interviews and comparative analyses. The report closes with conclusions and recommendations, in Chapter Five.

---

[6] Because the suppliers and users of the data are not wholly disinterested parties, we used data analysis and cross-service analysis to help shed light on potential issues.

CHAPTER TWO

The Air Force Specialty Classification Structure

Most of the features of the Air Force specialty-classification structure are similar for officer and enlisted personnel. The specialty classification structure provides a means of communicating about knowledge, skills, and abilities (KSA). It identifies the qualifications associated with various Air Force specialties, providing shorthand notations to describe the requisite KSA for most Air Force positions. It combines duties and tasks into cohesive job clusters that may be matched to personnel possessing the essential aptitudes, attributes, and qualifications. The structure facilitates training, information retrieval, counting, analyzing, and otherwise informing the Air Force of its human capital needs. It helps shape the system of work by providing labels and categories that are used to bundle tasks and duties into skill sets, occupations, positions, and jobs. This chapter discusses the specialty-classification concepts and tenets, describes the specialty-classification code schema, highlights differences between officer and enlisted codes, and provides illustrative uses for officer specialty codes.

Concepts and Tenets

The following concepts and tenets evolved from decades of identifying and matching the abilities of military personnel with job requirements.[1] One concept, *functional grouping* (see the discussion in the Fundamental Concepts subsection below), was documented in Air Force specialty-classification policy as early as 1954.[2] Basic tenets, such as providing visible career paths for officer and enlisted personnel, were added in more recent years. Collectively, these concepts and tenets serve as criteria for managing and evaluating changes to the classification structure—both officer and enlisted.

Fundamental Concepts

The Air Force military specialty-classification structure is rooted in two fundamental concepts: functional area grouping, incorporated into the earliest Air Force specialty-classification directives (Department of the Air Force [DAF], 1954) and practical specialization, integral to classification policy for more than 40 years (DAF, 1966).

1 Within this construct, *concepts* are considered the broad overarching ideas—for example, often service members will talk about concepts of operations. *Tenets* are principles or doctrines generally believed to be true.

2 The U.S. Air Force's system prior to 1954 was based on the U.S. Army's military occupational specialty (MOS) schema.

Functional Grouping. The concept of functional grouping provides a framework for procuring, training, and developing both specialized and broadly experienced personnel. Under this concept, occupational specialties and their corresponding jobs are clustered into relatively homogeneous groups. The clustering is based on similarity of functions, required knowledge, education, training, experience, ability, and other common criteria (DAF, 2006, p. 6). These Air Force specialties (AFSs) are further combined into broader and more general functional categories, labeled career fields. This framework helps ensure that, consistent with grade and skill level, airmen proficient in one position within a specialty should be capable of performing satisfactorily in any other position in the same specialty with minimum additional training.

Functional grouping provides a classification schema that remains relatively stable amid organizational changes. An organization, by its most basic definition, is a group of people working together to accomplish an overall, common goal or set of goals through a division of labor (Daft, 2007, p. 23). Large organizations, such as the Air Force, are continually modifying their organizational structures by changing business architectures and processes and experimenting with new organizational constructs as they seek to improve performance or adjust to internal and external constraints and opportunities. Functional grouping enables the Air Force to respond to these changes without major alterations to its specialty-classification schema. This stability aids other aspects of the human capital system, such as personnel assignments, training, and development.

Practical Specialization. No one person is likely to perform all of a specialty's tasks in any one job. When airmen meet the mandatory specialty and skill-level qualifications of their job, in reality they specialize in a practical subset of the specialty. Nevertheless, given the specialty's minimum and desired qualifications, airmen can be developed to perform all duties and responsibilities of the various jobs encountered throughout their career, with the least amount of additional training (DAF, 2006, p. 6). Practical specialization seeks to provide the degree of workforce specialization that is most efficient for almost all work situations.

Also, inherent in practical specialization is the notion of dividing specialties into sub-specialties when warranted. These subspecialties, delineated by alphabetical suffixes (shredouts), are used to identify specialization in specific types of equipment or functions. The amount of subdivision correlates positively to the heterogeneity within the specialty. Two officer examples are illustrative. Depending on rank, officer jobs within the security forces specialty (AFS 31P) are somewhat homogeneous; thus, there are no subspecialties (AFPC, 2006, pp. 81–82). By contrast, the jobs in the surgeon specialty (AFS 45S) may differ significantly (e.g., neurological versus thoracic), resulting in numerous subspecialties (AFPC, 2006, p. 155).

The concepts of functional grouping and practical specialization interact with each other to minimize the number of specialties with overlapping skill sets.

Basic Tenets

The Air Force's dynamic environment of changing missions, weapon systems, equipment, and technology often necessitates changes to specific specialties. Changes within a specialty normally have implications throughout the *human capital systems* (i.e., manpower planning, recruiting, training, assignments, promotions). Consequently, the Air Force propounded 16 tenets, shown in Table 2.1, to provide rigor and ensure that changes are evaluated by appropriate functional, personnel, and manpower agencies (DAF, 2006, pp. 55–58). The tenets preserve basic aspects of the specialty-classification structure and address four primary topics:

Table 2.1
Tenets of Air Force Specialty Classification

The classification system is established to • Identify requirements and the personnel required to fill those requirements. • Design AFSCs that make sense in the objective Air Force structure. • Use simple, clear, logical groupings. • Provide visible career paths for officer and enlisted personnel. • Maintain the ability to identify career fields, specialties, subspecialties, and skill levels. • Maintain the ability to identify special job requirements and positions, special duty identifiers (SDIs), and reporting identifiers (RIs). • Eliminate redundant identifiers. Do not duplicate other personnel data system (PDS) identifiers. • Group AFSCs functionally. • Maintain a balance of specialist versus generalist specialties to allow maximum efficiency and equity in assignment and promotion opportunities. • Not proliferate small-population specialties that adversely limit the ability to effectively manage the resource.
Specialty descriptions (contained in the respective *Air Force Officer Classification Directory* and *Enlisted Classification Directory*) for each occupational grouping will • Contain general occupation information (what most of the people do most of the time) and quantify the minimum requirements necessary to reasonably predict success in the specialty. • Be broad in scope to adequately portray all skill levels represented by the description and not contain a grade requirement. • Grade requirements are determined by Manpower, in conjunction with the Air Force Career Field Manager (AFCFM). • Have a standardized format, to maintain simplicity, clarity, and ease of publishing. • Generally be no more than 2 pages in length (does not include shredout descriptions when needed).
Each requested change to the classification system will be staffed with all affected agencies and any non-concurrence will be resolved before implementing.

SOURCE: Adapted from DAF, 2006, pp. 6–7.

- **Purpose.** The first tenet reiterates one purpose of the classification system: to identify requirements and the personnel qualified to fill those requirements.
- **Grouping guidelines.** Two tenets provide principles for clustering. One is to group AFSCs by the functions that they perform. The other tenet reminds users to use simple, clear, and logical groupings.
- **Criteria.** Many of the tenets provide criteria for evaluating change requests.
- **Administration.** Other tenets provide guidelines to facilitate the transmission of information and coordination.

These tenets have facilitated a classification structure that has systematically adapted to changes in skill requirements. But are they sufficient to guide the structure toward greater efficiency? We address this question in Chapter Four.

Air Force Specialty Code Schema

The specialty-classification structure consists of AFSCs, prefixes, suffixes, special-duty identifiers (SDIs), reporting identifiers (RIs), and special-experience identifiers (SEIs). The nucleus of this structure is the AFSC (DAF, 2006, p. 9). As shown in Figure 2.1, the officer AFSC consists of four alphanumeric digits and may include an alphabetic prefix and/or suffix (shredout).

For contrast, Figure 2.2 shows the enlisted AFSC, which consists of five alphanumeric digits and may include an alphabetic prefix and/or suffix (shredout). The differences between

Figure 2.1
Sample of Air Force Officer Specialty Code (Munitions and Missile Maintenance)

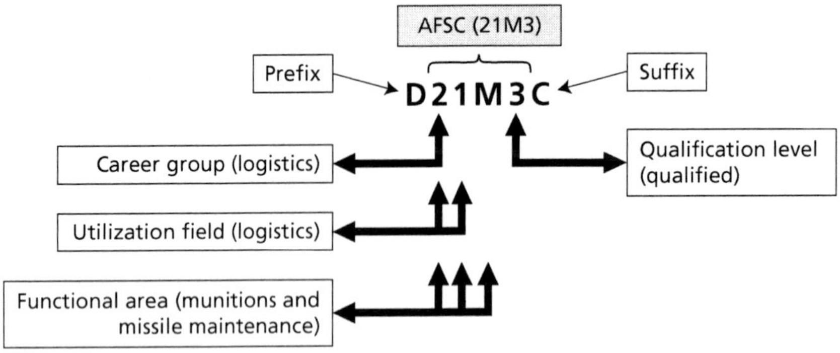

RAND *TR637-2.1*

Figure 2.2
Sample of Air Force Enlisted Specialty Code (Missile and Space Systems Electronic Maintenance)

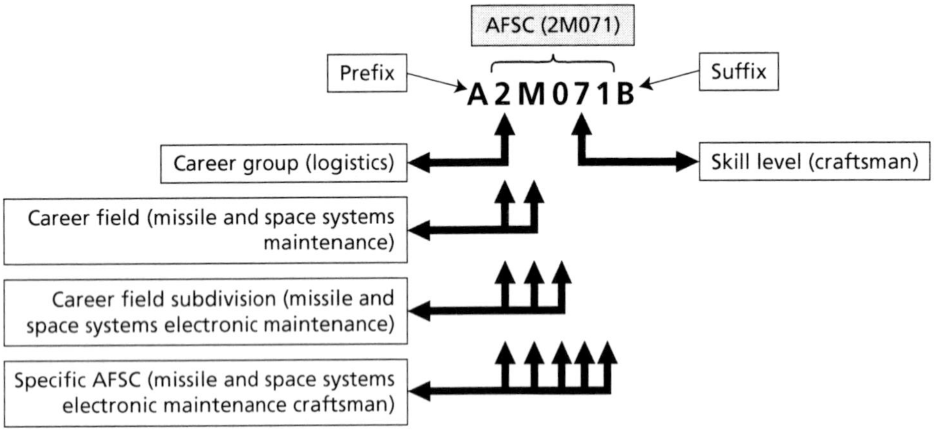

RAND *TR637-2.2*

the two coding schemes become important when identifying or tracking the number of specialties and subspecialties.

As shown in Table 2.2, excluding medical specialties, the six officer career groups (i.e., operations, logistics, support, professional, acquisition, and special investigations) are partitioned into 55 functional areas.[3] Sixty-five medical functional areas are distributed among health services, biomedical clinicians, biomedical specialists, medicine, surgery, nurse, dental, and aerospace medicine. As of 2006, the total was 120 functional areas, which excluded 33 special-duty and reporting identifiers.

Table 2.3 shows that in 2006, excluding medical, the six enlisted career groups (i.e., operations, logistics, support, professional, acquisition, and special investigations) were partitioned

---

[3] The first three digits are technically *functional areas*, although they are commonly referred to as *specialties* because most functional areas have only one specialty for officers. For enlisted personnel, the first three digits are technically the *career-field subdivision*. Also, the fifth digit is needed to make up what is commonly called a *specialty*.

Table 2.2
Air Force Officer Specialty Codes

Code	Specialty
Operations	
10C	Operations Commander
Pilot	
11B	Bomber Pilot
11E	Test Pilot
11F	Fighter Pilot
11G	Generalist Pilot
11H	Helicopter Pilot
11K	Trainer Pilot
11M	Mobility Pilot
11R	Recce/Surv/Elect Warfare Pilot
11S	Special Operations Pilot
11U	Remotely Operated Aircraft
Navigator	
12B	Bomber Navigator
12E	Test Navigator
12F	Fighter Navigator
12G	Generalist Navigator
12K	Trainer Navigator
12M	Mobility Navigator
12R	Recce/Surv/Elect Warfare Navigator
12S	Special Operations Navigator
12U	Remotely Operated Aircraft
Space, Missile, and C2	
13A	Astronaut
13B	Air Battle Manager
13D	Control and Recovery
13M	Airfield Operation
13S	Space & Missile
Intelligence	
14N	Intelligence
Weather	
15W	Weather
Operations Support	
16F	Regional Affairs Strategist
16G	Air Force Operations Staff Officer
16P	Political-Military Affairs Strategist
16R	Planning & Programming
Logistics	
20C	Logistics Commander
Logistics	
21A	Aircraft Maintenance
21M	Munitions and Missile Maintenance
21R	Logistics Readiness
Support	
30C	Support Commander
Security Forces	
31P	Security Forces
Civil Engineering	
32E	Civil Engineer
Communications	
33C	Communications Commander
33S	Communications and Information
Services	
34M	Services
Public Affairs	
35B	Band
35P	Public Affairs
Manpower-Personnel	
37F	Manpower-Personnel
Medical	
40C	Medical Commander
Health Services	
41A	Health Services Administrator
Biomedical Clinicians	
42B	Physical Therapist
42E	Optometrist
42F	Podiatrist
42G	Physician Assistant
42N	Audiology/Speech Pathologist
42P	Clinical Psychologist
42S	Clinical Social Worker
42T	Occupational Therapist
Biomedical Specialists	
43A	Aerospace Physiologist
43B	Biomedical Scientist
43D	Dietitian
43E	Bioenvironmental Engineer
43H	Public Health
43M	Medical Entomologist
43P	Pharmacist
43T	Biomedical Laboratory
43V	Veterinary Clinician
43Y	Health Physicist
Medicine	
44A	Chief, Hospital/Clinic Services
44B	Preventive Medicine
44D	Pathologist
44E	Emergency Services Physician
44F	Family Physician
44G	General Practice Physician
44H	Nuclear Medicine Physician
44J	Clinical Geneticist
44K	Pediatrician
44M	Internist
44N	Neurologist
44P	Psychiatrist
44R	Diagnostic Radiologist
44S	Dermatologist
44T	Radiotherapist
44U	Occupational Medicine
44Y	Critical Care Medicine
44Z	Allergist
Surgery	
45A	Anesthesiologist
45B	Orthopedic Surgeon
45E	Ophthalmologist
45G	OB/GYN
45N	Otorhinolaryngologist
45P	Physical Medicine Physician
45S	Surgeon
45U	Urologist
Nurse	
46A	Nurse Administrator
46F	Flight Nurse
46G	Nurse-Midwife
46M	Nurse Anesthetist
46N	Clinical Nurse
46P	Mental Health Nurse
46S	Operating Room Nurse
Dental	
47B	Orthodontist
47D	Oral and Maxillofacial Pathologist
47E	Endodontist
47G	Dentist
47H	Periodontist
47K	Pediatric Dentist
47P	Prosthodontist
47S	Oral Surgeon
Aerospace Medicine	
48A	Aerospace Medicine Specialist
48G	General Medical Officer (GMO)
48R	Residency Trained Flight Surgeon
48V	Pilot-Physician
Professional	
Law	
51J	Judge Advocate
Chaplain	
52R	Chaplain
Acquisition	
Command	
60C	Program Director
Scientific Research & Development	
61S	Scientist
Developmental Engineer	
62E	Developmental Engineer
Acquisition	
63A	Acquisition Manager
Contracting	
64P	Contracting
Finance	
65A	Auditor
65F	Financial Management
65W	Cost Analysis
Special Investigations	
71S	Special Investigator
Special Duty Identifiers	
80C	Commander, Cadet Squadron, USAFA
81C	Training Commander, OTS
81T	Instructor
82A	Academic Program Manager
83R	Recruiting Service
84H	Historian
85G	USAF Honor Guard
86M	Operations Management
86P	Command and Control
87G	Inspector General
88A	Aide-de-Camp
Reporting Identifiers	
90G	General Officer
91C	Commander
91W	Wing Commander
92J0	Nondesignated Lawyer
92J1	AFROTC Educational Delay–Law
92J2	Funded Legal Ed Program Law Stude
92J3	Excess Leave Law Student
92M0	Heath Professions Scholarship Program (HPSP) Medical Student
92M1	Uniformed Services University of Health Sciences Student
92M2	HPSP Biomedical Science Student
92R	Chaplain Candidate
92S	Student Officer Authorization
92T0	Pilot Trainee
92T1	Navigator Trainee
92T2	Air Battle Manager Trainee
93P	Patient
94N	Nuclear Weapons Custodian
95A	Non- Extended Active Duty USAFR Academy/CAP Liaison Officer
96D	Off not Avail in awarded AFSC for ca
96U	Unclassified Officer
96V	Unallotted
97E	Executive Officer Above Wing Level

SOURCE: Adapted from *Air Force Quick Reference Guide for Officer Air Force Specialty Codes*, October 31, 2006 (Attachment 2 of the *Air Force Officer Classification Directory* [DAF, 2007]).
NOTES: Recce/Surv/Elect = reconnaissance/surveillance/electronic; USAFA = U.S. Air Force Academy; OTS = Officer Training School; HPSP = Health Professions Scholarship Program.

into 31 career fields. There were 15 medical and dental career fields. Excluding combinations associated with skill codes, the 46 career fields are further divided into 139 specific AFSCs. In addition, there were 26 special-duty and reporting identifiers.

Table 2.3
Air Force Enlisted Specialty Codes

Operations	
Aircrew Operations	
1A0X1	In-Flight Refueling
1A1X1	Flight Engineer
1A2X1	Loadmaster
1A3X1	Airborne Mission Systems
1A4X1	Airborne Battle Management
1A6X1	Flight Attendant
1A7X1	Aerial Gunner
1A8X1	Airborne Cryptologic Linguist
Command Control Systems Operations	
1C0X2	Aviation Resource Management
1C1X1	Air Traffic Control
1C2X1	Combat Control
1C3X1	Command Post
1C4X1	Tactical Air Control Party (TACP)
1C5X1	Aerospace Control and Warning Systems
1C6X1	Space Systems Operations
1C7X1	Airfield Management
Intelligence	
1N0X1	Intelligence Applications
1N1X1	Imagery Analysis
1N2X1	Com Signals Intelligence
1N3X1	Germanic Cryptologic Linguist
1N3X2	Romance Cryptologic Linguist
1N3X3	Slavic Cryptologic Linguist
1N3X4	Far East Cryptologic Linguist
1N3X5	Mid-East Cryptologic Linguist
1N3X6	African Cryptologic Linguist
1N3X7	Turkic Cryptologic Linguist
1N3X8	Polynesian Cryptologic Linguist
1N3X9	Indo-Iranian Cryptologic Linguist
1N4X1	Network Intelligence Analyst
1N5X1	Electronic Signals Intelligence Exploitation
1N6X1	Electronic System Security Assessment
Safety	
1S0X1	Safety
Aircrew Protection	
1T0X1	Survival, Evasion, Resistance, and Escape
1T1X1	Aircrew Life Support
1T2X1	Pararescue
Weather	
1W0X1	Weather
Logistics	
Aerospace Maintenance	
2A0X1	Avionics Test Station and Components
2A3X1	A-10, F-15, & U-2 Avionics Systems
2A3X2	F-16, F-117, RQ-1, CV-22 Avionic Systems
2A3X3	Tactical Aircraft Maintenance
2A5X1	Aerospace Maintenance
2A5X2	Helicopter Maintenance
2A5X3	Integrated Avionics Systems
2A6X1	Aerospace Propulsion
2A6X2	Aerospace Ground Equipment
2A6X3	Aircrew Egress Systems
2A6X4	Aircraft Fuel Systems
2A6X5	Aircraft Hydraulic Systems
2A6X6	Aircraft Electrical and Environmental Sys
2A7X1	Aircraft Metals Technology
2A7X2	Nondestructive Inspection
2A7X3	Aircraft Structural Maintenance
2A7X4	Survival Equipment
Comm-Elec/Wire Systems Maintenance	
2E0X1	Ground Radar Systems
2E1X1	Satellite, Wideband, and Telemetry Systems
2E1X2	Airfield Systems
2E1X3	Ground Radio Communications
2E1X4	Visual Imagery and Intrusion Detection Sys
2E2X1	Com, Network, Switching & Crypto Sys
2E6X2	Comm Cable and Antenna Systems
2E6X3	Voice Network Systems
Fuels	
2F0X1	Fuels
Logistics Plans	
2G0X1	Logistics Plans
Missile Maintenance	
2M0X1	Missile and Space Systems Elect Mx
2M0X2	Missile and Space Systems Maintenance
2M0X3	Missile and Space Facilities
Precision Measurement	
2P0X1	Precision Measurement Equipment Lab
Maintenance Management	
2R0X1	Maintenance Management Analyst
2R1X1	Maintenance Production
Material Management	
2S0X1	Material Management
Transportation	
2T0X1	Traffic Management
2T1X1	Vehicle Operations
2T2X1	Air Transportation
Vehicle Maintenance	
2T3X1	Vehicle and Vehicular Equipment Mx
2T3X2	Special Vehicle Maintenance
2T3X5	Vehicle Body Maintenance
2T3X7	Vehicle Management & Analysis
Munitions & Weapons	
2W0X1	Munitions Systems
2W1X1	Aircraft Armament Systems
2W2X1	Nuclear Weapons
Support	
Information Management	
3A0X1	Information Management
Communication-Computer Systems	
3C0X1	Comm-Computer Systems Operations
3C0X2	Comm-Computer Systems Programming
3C1X1	Radio Communications Systems
3C1X2	Electromagnetic Spectrum Management
3C2X1	Communication-Computer Systems Control
3C3X1	Comm-Comp Sys Planning & Implementation
Civil Engineering	
3E0X1	Electrical Systems
3E0X2	Electrical Power Production
3E1X1	Heating, Ventilation, AC, & Refrigeration
3E2X1	Pavement and Construction Equipment
3E3X1	Structural
3E4X1	Utilities Systems
3E4X2	Liquid Fuel Systems Maintenance
3E4X3	Pest Management
3E5X1	Engineering
3E6X1	Operations Management
3E7X1	Fire Protection
3E8X1	Explosive Ordnance Disposal
3E9X1	Readiness
Historian	
3H0X1	Historian
Services	
3M0X1	Services
Public Affairs	
3N0X1	Public Affairs
3N0X2	Radio and Television Broadcasting
3N1X1	Regional Band
3N2X1	Premier Band
Security Forces	
3P0X1	Security Forces
Mission Support	
3S0X1	Personnel
3S1X1	Military Equal Opportunity
3S2X1	Education and Training
3S3X1	Manpower
Multimedia	
3V0X1	Graphic Arts
3V0X2	Still Photography
3V0X3	Video
Medical	
4A0X1	Health Services Management
4A1X1	Medical Materiel
4A2X1	Biomedical Equipment
4B0X1	Bioenvironmental Engineering
4C0X1	Mental Health Service
4D0X1	Diet Therapy
4E0X1	Public Health
4H0X1	Cardiopulmonary Laboratory
4J0X2	Physical Medicine
4M0X1	Aerospace Physiology
4N0X1	Aerospace Medical Service
4N1X1	Surgical Service
4P0X1	Pharmacy
4R0X1	Diagnostic Imaging
4T0X1	Medical Laboratory
4T0X2	Histopathology
4U0X1	Orthotic
4V0X1	Ophthalmic
Dental	
4Y0X1	Dental Assistant
4Y0X2	Dental Laboratory
Professional	
Legal	
5J0X1	Paralegal
Chaplain Service Support	
5R0X1	Chaplain Assistant
Acquisition	
Contracting	
6C0X1	Contracting
Financial	
6F0X1	Financial Management & Comptroller
Special Investigations	
7S0X1	Special Investigations
Special Duty Identifiers	
8A100	Career Assistance Advisor
8A200	Enlisted Aide
8B000	Military Training Instructor
8B100	Military Training Leader
8B200	Academy Military Training NCO
8C000	Family Support Center
8D000	Linguist Debriefer
8E000	Research and Development Craftsman
8F000	First Sergeant
8G000	Honor Guard
8J000	Correctional Custody Supervisor
8M000	Postal Specialist
8P000	Courier
8P100	Defense Attaché Specialist
8R000	Enlisted Accessions Recruiter
8R200	Second-Tier Recruiter
8R300	Third-Tier Recruiter
8S000	Missile Facility Manager
8T000	Professional Military Education Instructor
Reporting Identifiers	
9A000	Awaiting Retrain-Reasons beyond Control
9A100	Awaiting Retrain - Reasons within Control
9A200	Awaiting Discharge/Separation/Retirement for Reasons Within Their Control
9A300	Awaiting Discharge/Separation/Retirement for Reasons Beyond Their Control
9C000	CMSgt of the Air Force
9D000	Dormitory Manager
9E000	Command Chief Master Sergeant
9F000	First Term Airmen Center
9G100	Group Superintendent
9J000	Prisoner
9L000	Interpreter/Translator
9P000	Patient
9R000	Civil Air Patrol (CAP)-USAF Reserve Assistance NCOs
9S100	Technical Applications Specialist
9T000	Basic Enlisted Airman
9T100	Officer Trainee
9T200	Pre-Cadet Assignee
9U000	Ineligible for Local Utilization
9U100	Unallotted Airman

SOURCE: Adapted from *Air Force Quick Reference Guide for Enlisted Air Force Specialty Codes*, October 31, 2006 (Attachment 2 of the *Air Force Classification Directory* [DAF, 2007]).

Prefixes and Suffixes

Quite often, AFSCs are augmented with prefixes and suffixes. *Prefixes* are used to identify an ability, skill, or special qualification that is not restricted to a single functional area or career field. For example, in Figure 2.1, the prefix “D” refers to Advanced Logistics Officer Course graduates. It may be used with AFSCs from three functional areas: aircraft maintenance (AFSC 21A), munitions and missile maintenance (AFSC 21M), and logistics readiness (AFSC 21R).

Suffixes, commonly called shredouts, are restricted to a single functional area or career field and relate to specific equipment or functions. For officers, when appropriate, a suffix may be added to the four-digit AFSC. Again referring to Figure 2.1, adding a "C" in this example indicates that this munitions and missile maintenance officer has nuclear experience or that the position requires a munitions and missile officer with nuclear experience. Suffixes are used in a similar manner for enlisted specialties, except that they are added to the five-digit AFSC as shown in Figure 2.2.

Special-Duty Identifiers (SDIs)

SDIs resemble other AFSCs, but the first numeric digit is always an "8" and there are no skill or qualification levels. They are used to identify positions and people performing duties that are not clearly within a specific career field. The code "80C" would be used for the commander of a cadet squadron at the Air Force Academy. The code "8B2" would be used for an Academy military training noncommissioned officer (NCO). Although the duties are not within a specific career field, general tasks and responsibilities are outlined in a specialty description. As shown in Tables 2.2 and 2.3, there are 11 officer SDIs and 19 enlisted SDIs.

Reporting Identifiers (RIs)

RIs also resemble other AFSCs, but the first numeric digit is always a "9" and there are no skill or qualification levels. They are used to identify people and/or positions that are not otherwise identifiable in the classification structure. For example, the code "92J" would be used for a student in a sponsored legal program (e.g., 92J1—AFROTC educational delay law student, 92J3—Excess Leave Law Student). The code "9A300" would be used for an enlisted person awaiting discharge/separation/retirement for reasons beyond their control. Although exceptions exist, RIs are primarily intended to identify people and/or positions for which specific job descriptions are impractical. Two examples are an officer awaiting specialty classification (96U) and a hospitalized officer patient (93P).

Special-Experience Identifiers (SEIs)

SEIs are a set of three-digit codes used to identify special experience and training not otherwise identified in the personnel and manpower data systems. They are components of the specialty classification structure; however, they are not substitutes for AFSCs, suffixes, prefixes, special-duty identifiers, reporting identifiers, personnel processing codes, or professional specialty course codes (DAF, 2006, p. 26). They provide a means to track individuals and identify positions requiring or providing unique experience or training that would otherwise be lost. They also provide a method to rapidly identify an already-experienced resource to meet unique circumstances, contingency requirements, or management needs.

SEIs are alphanumeric, consisting of an activity code (first character) and an experience set (last two characters). Let us consider the code "OCE." The activity code "O" denotes officers directly involved in the employment of weapon and supporting systems to accomplish the primary operational mission of the Air Force. The two remaining characters identify a particular system, level of experience, or the type of experience. In this example, the experience set "CE" denotes an officer functioning in mission-ready or operational-ready status in the duty of air surveillance officer or sensor system manager in Airborne Warning and Control System

(AWACS), in any mobile tactical air control radar system, or in a fixed air defense command and control facility. By combining the activity codes with the experience sets, over 7,200 separate SEIs are possible.[4] However, a query of the manpower and personnel data systems revealed that less than 600 codes are used routinely.

Unlike officer SEIs, most enlisted SEIs are strictly numeric.[5] Also, they are not composed of activity codes and experience sets. Instead, each three-digit code has a specific meaning. The enlisted SEI codes, their titles, and their criteria are listed in Section III of the Air Force Enlisted Classification Directory (AFECD). The vast majority of enlisted SEIs are associated with specific AFSCs. Very few enlisted SEIs may be used with multiple AFSCs.

Illustrative Uses

The Air Force's human capital system is composed of three principal subsystems: manpower, personnel, and training.[6] The manpower subsystem focuses on determining the demand for and rationing of human capital; the personnel subsystem focuses on managing the supply of human capital; and the training subsystem focuses on developing human capital. The Air Force specialty codes provide a language that facilitates communication within and across these subsystems. The following examples illustrate how critical they are to the human capital system.

Manpower

Human capital management cannot take place without a defined requirement. The Air Force uses many tools to determine its officer requirements, including manpower standards, crew ratios, programming factors, and staffing patterns. Regardless of the tool, the objective is to specify the *requirement* in terms of quantity, specialty codes, and measures of experience (normally, skill levels and/or qualifications and grade). In the aggregate, requirements typically exceed available funding and end strength (DAF, 2003, pp. 19–20). Therefore, requirements get prioritized—sometimes *de facto*.[7] The commands transmit these priorities to the rest of the Air Force by updating unit manpower documents (UMDs) with the appropriate organization, specialty codes, grade, program element, etc.

Personnel

The primary objective for the personnel subsystem is to provide unit commanders with the best mix of mission-ready people given the status of available resources. The Air Force uses a centralized military assignment process to distribute people in accordance with unit needs and in compliance with laws and directives, ensuring that assignments are equitable and cost-

[4] Any one of the 16 activity codes may be combined with any one of 451 experience sets, resulting in 7,216 possible SEI codes. A list of the activity codes and experience sets, as of October 31, 2006, is provided in Appendix B.

[5] The Intelligence Community uses a three-digit alphanumeric code. The first digit is numeric, and the two remaining digits are alphabetic characters.

[6] For a comprehensive discussion of the Air Force human capital system, see Chapter Two in Conley et al., 2006.

[7] For example, Logistics Composite Model (LCOM) aircraft-maintenance requirements may have been validated as necessary to accomplish the mission; however, if no funding is available, the local unit or MAJCOM must determine which specific positions will not be included in the unit's funded manpower entitlements.

effective, and maintaining personnel accountability (DAF, 2005, p. 1).[8] People are distributed as equitably as possible between major commands (or the equivalent) within a specialty and grade to meet overall AF needs. Using UMDs, assignment managers seek to come as close as possible to providing commanders with the right number of skilled people in the proper specialty and grade to perform their missions.

To estimate future needs, workforce sustainment models[9] use historical retention, cross-flow behavior,[10] and authorized manpower levels to project personnel-inventory targets for each year of service. For nonrated line (NRL) officers,[11] the sustainment process is based on the needs of each specialty and is determined by weighing the funded manpower authorizations, the number of personnel performing duties in the specialty, the number of personnel possessing the core AFSC who are working outside the specialty (i.e., special duty, in-residence professional military education, or graduate school), the retention within the specialty, and the career field health[12] (DAF, 2004b, p. 3). Sustainment needs generate accession requirements, academic targets, and acceptable ranges for accessions by AFSC for future fiscal years.

Training

The purpose of Air Force training is to ensure that each individual is prepared to meet Air Force mission requirements. Directed training[13] supports the trained personnel requirements (TPRs) needed to replenish and balance the force (i.e., to ensure that enough trained personnel are in each specialty to accomplish the Air Force mission). Normally, officers must complete the training requirements listed in the specialty description contained in the *Air Force Officer Classification Directory* (for example, AFPC, 2006), the *Career Field Education and Training Plan* (CFETP) (included in DAF, 2004a)[14] or the *Officer Professional Development Plan* (a discussion of the responsibilities of individuals, units, etc., is given in DAF, 2004a, p. 4).

Adequate training and timely progression from entry level to the intermediate level or qualified level play an important role in the Air Force's ability to accomplish its mission. Air Education and Training Command (AETC) pipeline training managers[15] make sure that training programs support specialty requirements.

---

[8] The Air Force must be able to account for all of its personnel by duty status, duty location, etc., which it refers to as *personnel accountability*.

[9] *Sustainment models* estimate the flow (accessions, cross-flows, separations, retirements, etc.) needed to maintain the personnel levels required to accomplish the Air Force missions.

[10] *Cross-flow behavior* is people cross-training into other career fields.

[11] Air Force line officers are divided into rated and nonrated. *Rated line officers* are flying-related: pilots, navigators, or air battle managers. *Nonrated line officers* fall into two categories: nonrated operations, such as intelligence or weather, and nonrated support, such as maintenance, logistics, or communications.

[12] One indicator of *career field health* is how well the actual people inventory compares with the manpower requirements by skill, grade, etc.

[13] *Directed training* is training the Air Force pays for because it is needed to replenish the force. It includes initial-skills training, lateral training, and professional military education (PME).

[14] Officer CFETPs are used only when the Air Force Career Field Manager (AFCFM) determines that the Officer Career Development Plan does not adequately identify training needs. It serves as a road map for career progression and outlines requirements that must be satisfied at appropriate points throughout the career path.

[15] *Pipeline training managers* are training managers in AETC who are responsible for cradle-to-grave management of initial-skills formal courses (*pipelines*) and for performing MAJCOM staff-level training management.

This chapter has provided a synopsis of the nuts and bolts of the Air Force specialty classification structure, which is rooted in concepts that have been refined through decades of experience in matching people with positions. The structure has remained relatively stable while incrementally responding to changing missions, new technologies, and reengineered processes.

CHAPTER THREE

Past and Future Changes

The specialty-classification structure is part of the human capital infrastructure. Analogous to a transportation system, it serves both global and local interests. As with other infrastructure systems, changes most often occur locally (i.e., within communities), incrementally, and build on existing foundations. However, global changes are infrequent and usually take several years to implement.

Two Prominent Comprehensive Studies

During the past 60 years, the Air Force has conducted two comprehensive evaluations of its specialty-classification structure. These evaluations produced global changes that permeated every aspect of its operations.

Breaking from the Army

During the transition from the United States Army Air Corps to the United States Air Force, the specialty-classification structure retained its Army heritage as military occupational specialty (MOS) codes. In fact, before 1950, Air Force enlisted personnel were still called "soldiers."[1] In 1951, a three-year study, called "Operation Searchlight," was initiated (Headquarters U.S. Air Force, Office of the Deputy Chief of Staff, Personnel, 1951). Air Force leaders realized that the Army system no longer fit the newly independent service, with its many highly technical jobs and few enlisted combat specialties.[2] This study coalesced efforts of 200 specialty-classification experts from the other military branches, civilian industry, and other governmental agencies to develop a classification structure appropriate for the Air Force.[3]

In 1954, the new specialty structure was implemented (DAF, 1954). It provided a new coding scheme, eliminated unneeded Army codes, and defined new technology-based specialties. Headquarters USAF revised the tables of organization to reflect the changes. Major commands revised non–table-of-organization documents to reflect the changes. Individual qualifi-

---

[1] On February 20, 1950, Gen Hoyt S. Vandenberg directed that Air Force enlisted personnel be called "airmen" to distinguish them from "soldiers" and "sailors" (DAF, 1950).

[2] When the Air Force became independent in 1947, it adopted a "One Air Force" organization, in which officers were commissioned into, and enlisted personnel were members of, the Air Force. Although people may perform specialized jobs, they were all part of "One Air Force," not a specialized branch or corps, which had been a characteristic of the Army specialty structure (Mitchell, 1996).

[3] During this period, studies were being conducted to change the enlisted grade structure. These changes were intertwined with plans for improving the quality of NCO leadership (Grandstaff, 1997).

cations were reviewed, and people were classified in an appropriate new specialty. The specialty structure that was implemented then remained, for all practical purposes, until an October 1993 classification restructuring.

The 1993 Specialty Classification Restructuring

The end of the Cold War in 1989–1991 precipitated a severe drawdown in military forces. Recognizing the need to streamline, the Air Force soon underwent the most complete reorganization since its establishment. It consolidated from 13 to eight major commands, inactivated 64 wings or equivalents, and closed numerous bases. Amid the streamlining, 1993 was dubbed the "Year of Training," with the Air Education and Training Command being formed via a merger of Air Training Command and the Air University, and with all initial training of weapon-system aircrew being transferred from Air Combat Command (ACC) and Air Mobility Command (AMC) to AETC. In addition, the specialty-code structure and the associated training for every officer and enlisted career field were reviewed and revised.

The specialty-restructure objectives were to better match the specialties with the needs of the restructured Air Force and to realign career fields that had become fragmented (Boles, 1993). During the process,

- both officer and enlisted systems were to be modernized.
- the number of people in narrow specialties was to be reduced by combining similar specialties.
- clearer pictures of natural groups were to be developed by aligning officer and enlisted AFSCs by functional area and mirroring the first character.
- more generalists were to be created, affording increased flexibility.

The restructuring reduced the number of officer AFSCs to 123 from 216, and enlisted AFSCs to 176 from 203. Necessary training revisions were made as career paths were reviewed and utilization and training workshops were held. The revamped specialty-classification structure was implemented in October 1993, and salient features have remained essentially unchanged.

The System Rarely Pauses

While major changes have been rare, the specialty structure is being tweaked continually.

Changes Within Communities

The overall structure of the specialty codes has remained relatively stable since 1993, but specialty content and details are frequently updated. Additionally, as Figure 3.1 shows, it is not uncommon for entire specialties to be added or deleted. Establishing new AFSCs or revising existing ones usually requires changes to manning documents and training courses and reevaluating individual qualifications; consequently, the specialty codes are updated on a quarterly cycle (DAF, 2006, p. 52).[4]

---

[4] Prior to 2007, the specialty codes were updated only twice a year.

During the period 1994 to 2006, functional-area restructuring deleted 18 specialties and created 18 new specialties. For instance, restructuring within the logistics community reduced the number of officer specialties from eight to three (21A—aircraft maintenance, 21M—munitions and missile maintenance, 21—logistics readiness). As another example of restructuring, airlift pilots (11A) and tanker pilots (11T) were grouped to become mobility pilots (11M) in 2004. In contrast to these reductions in specialties, in 2003 a new specialty was created for remotely operated aircraft (11U). The watershed years for deleting suffixes were 2001 and 2002.[5] In 2001, 211 suffixes were eliminated: 57 medical, 35 logistics, 35 acquisition, 29 space, missile, and C2, 11 communication/information, and 44 others. In 2002, 47 were eliminated: 31 pilot, 12 navigator, and 4 logistics.

Figure 3.1 suggests that the number of officer specialties shrinks and expands as warranted, and that the overall trend is a reduction in the aggregate number.

Total Number of AFSCs Being Reduced Further

During fall 2006, the Air Force Chief of Staff tasked the Deputy Chief of Staff for Manpower and Personnel to lead a group chartered to determine the correct blend, or combination, of AFSCs. Similarly to the 1993 endeavor, one of the objectives was to reduce the number of specialties. The group concluded that the specialty structure was sound, but that it has a propensity toward a high degree of specialization driven by equipment, technology, and/or mission. Working with the functional managers and functional authorities,[6] the group documented over 100 candidates to consider for possible consolidation or elimination.

Figure 3.1
Air Force Officer AFSC Changes (1994 to 2006)

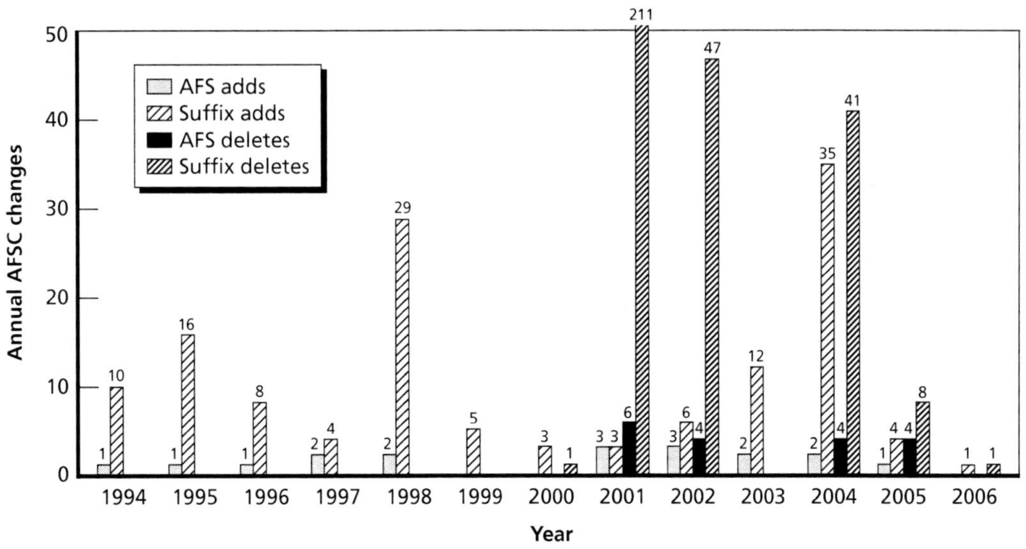

RAND *TR637-3.1*

---

[5] In 2001 and 2002, several organizational and process-reengineering initiatives included combining specific specialties. For example, the CSAF's Logistics Review fostered the merger of supply and transportation specialties. An Air Mobility Command initiative combined the tanker and airlift specialties into a mobility specialty.

[6] The *functional authority* provides corporate Air Force perspective on institutional requirements and force management and development. Functional authorities are supported by functional managers, who are supported by career-field managers.

Table 3.1 shows the possible adjustments by career group. The number of career fields is unchanged: 29 for officers and 46 for enlisted personnel. Within the officer career fields, 16 AFSCs could be considered for elimination. Within the enlisted career fields, 92 AFSCs could be considered for elimination. The potential adjustments in operations included merging flight engineers, load masters, and flight attendants, as well as the restructuring associated with establishing a battlefield airman specialty.[7] The logistics adjustments included consolidating several aircraft maintenance specialties and adding new ones for low-observable surfaces. The logistics adjustments also included merging vehicle-equipment and vehicle-body maintenance. The support adjustments included restructuring the communication/computer specialties, merging Manpower and Personnel with Services, merging liquid fuels and utilities systems, and consolidating several civil engineering subspecialties. The medical adjustments stem from consolidating several subspecialties.

As this group dealt with the blend of AFSCs, a broader issue began to emerge: processes for updating the specialty-classification structure are relatively unresponsive to mission changes. As described below, this issue is now being addressed as an AFSO21 initiative.[8]

Toward a More Responsive Specialty-Change Process

As discussed in Chapter Two, the specialty-classification structure has implications for every part of human capital management. As a result, the coordination process for changes is lengthy and implementation may take years. New missions are emerging, and technology and pro-

Table 3.1
Tally of Possible AFSC Consolidations or Eliminations

	Career Fields		Air Force Specialty Codes			
			Officer		Enlisted	
Career Groups	Officer	Enlisted	Baseline	Adj	Baseline	Adj
1. Operations	6	6	232	0	132	–58
2. Logistics	1	11	5	0	84	–20
3. Support	6	9	19	–11	54	–12
4. Medical	8	15	195	–8	31	–2
5. Professional	2	2	8	0	2	0
6. Acquisition	5	2	18	3	2	0
7. OSI	1	1	1	0	1	0
Subtotal	29	46	478	–16	306	–92
8. Special Duty			11	0	19	0
9. Reporting Identifiers			22	0	19	0
Total			511	–16	344	–92

NOTE: Adj = adjustments.

[7] This restructuring involved deleting old specialties and creating new ones (variation of 1Bxxx) and making adjustments to training courses to include the 376th Air Expeditionary Wing.

[8] Air Force Smart Operations 21, commonly known as AFSO21, was created to look at process improvement across the Air Force.

cesses are changing faster than the classification structure can respond. The Air Force does not have a centralized process to identify threats and situations requiring AFSC restructuring; instead, it relies on functional managers to individually identify required changes. Nor do the policies sufficiently address enterprise-wide manpower and personnel priorities, boundaries, and guidance to facilitate AFSC restructuring.

The *AFSO21 initiative* seeks to remedy the lack of responsiveness by developing specialty-change processes that are triggered by significant changes in missions, manpower, technology, and/or processes. The output of these processes would be AFSC change proposals[9] that are ready for the implementation process. If the initiative is successful, it should facilitate the necessary adjustments to its recruiting, classification, training, assignment, and education systems to more responsively produce personnel to meet Air Force needs.

The Role of Functional Communities

For the near term, the vast majority of changes to the specialty structure will be driven by the functional communities. Here are some officer examples of recent or upcoming changes:

Fighter Pilots. The April 2007 *Air Force Officer Classification Directory* (AFOCD) does not contain a suffix for F-35 fighter pilots. The aircraft are expected to begin entering the Air Force inventory by 2010, with pilot training starting early that year. A new suffix for the F-35 will be added shortly to the fighter pilot AFS.

Manpower and Personnel Merger with Services. The Personnel community began transforming itself in 2003 by redesigning its personnel services delivery. The objectives were to reduce the transactional footprint at base level through reachback[10] and technology, to reduce duplication between various levels of higher headquarters-staff activities, and to achieve Manpower savings. Later, Manpower and Personnel specialties and organizations were merged in an effort to provide cradle-to-grave processes for human resource management. Currently, Services organizations are being merged with Manpower and Personnel.

The latest structure is intended to streamline processes, maximize customer service, and cut the costs of maintaining separate organizations. It places Manpower, Personnel, and Services capabilities under one commander or director. In conjunction with the organizational changes, the Manpower and Personnel officer specialties were previously merged, and the Services officer specialty will soon be included as well.

Civil Engineering. The Civil Engineering community is exploring the feasibility of using one AFSC for all civil engineers. Doing so would delete the suffixes for architects, readiness non-engineer, electrical, mechanical, explosive ordnance disposal (EOD) engineer, and environmental. In lieu of suffixes, SEIs would be established to track specific engineer requirements and capabilities.

Medical. The medical community has a long history of expanding and contracting its subspecialties as needed. Current plans include merging biomedical engineers and health physicists and, possibly, deleting suffixes for veterinary clinicians and multiorgan transplant surgeons.

---

[9] *Change proposals* describe updated duties and responsibilities, updated specialty qualifications, assessments of training effects, etc. This process currently takes 2 or 3 years.

[10] The term *reachback* is used here to connote redesigned personnel processes and organizations that provide 24-hour-a-day, 7-day-a-week customer service from an enhanced central Contact Center via Web-based applications.

More Changes Are Emerging

Both internal and external factors may drive significant changes. In addition to the ongoing changes cited above, more changes are on the horizon. The changes discussed below may be indicative of more-fundamental changes yet to come.

Air Force Cyber Activities

The Air Force's envisioned cyber[11] mission is to provide combat-ready forces trained and equipped to conduct sustained global operations in and through cyberspace, fully integrated with air and space operations (Lord, 2007, p. 2). Its goal is to provide robust, survivable access to cyberspace with offensive and defensive capabilities that ensure the ability to maintain freedom of action in and through air, space, and cyberspace despite adversary actions, for U.S. friends and allies, and that deny the same to U.S. adversaries. Perhaps one of the more critical tasks is to develop a cadre of professionals with cyberspace skills in electronic warfare, network warfare, and network operations with competencies for exercising core cyberspace capabilities—Using the Domain (Cyberspace Attack and Force Enhancement); Controlling the Domain (Cyberspace Defensive Operations and Cyberspace Offensive Counteractions); and Establishing the Domain (Global Expeditionary Cyberspace Operations, Command and Control Network and Security Operations, and Cyberspace Civil Support Operations)—across the full range of military operations.

Much as for the early years of Air Force Space Command, the Air Force has to determine the specialty implications of the emerging mission.[12] New specialty codes are in the coordination-and-approval process. For officers, the specialties may encompass both electronic warfare and cyber warfare. For the enlisted force, they may include communications technology, systems management, airborne systems, and control systems. *The new specialties mean the entire training regime for cyber and electronic warfare personnel must be examined.* Training pipelines must be established, skills-transition actions must be planned, and career-development plans must be fleshed out.

Defense Integrated Military Human Resources System (DIMHRS)

When implemented, DIMHRS is envisioned as a comprehensive, Web-based system integrating military personnel and pay processes and data for the Army and Air Force to include active duty, Reserve, and National Guard components.[13] DIMHRS could be the catalyst for the most dramatic change in the specialty structure since 1993. The first phase is expected to roll out in 2009, incorporating the personnel and pay functions. Subsequent phases will incorporate manpower and training functions, leading to a single integrated human resources system.

---

[11] *Cyberspace* is a global domain within the information environment consisting of the interdependent network of information-technology infrastructures, including the Internet, telecommunications networks, computer systems, and embedded processors and controllers.

[12] PAF has been assisting the Air Force with assessing the specialty implications.

[13] In November 2007, the Navy and Marine Corps indicated that they will move to DIMHRS after all, but they did not specify when. As of June 2007, the Navy has expressed a preference for the Marine Corps Total Force System (MCTFS). If MCTFS had been adopted by the Navy and Marine Corps, it was expected to fully integrate with DIMHRS.

In conjunction with implementing DIMHRS, *processes are being reengineered* to help achieve the following benefits:[14]

- Streamline and automate processes—one-time data entry, automatically updating information in all required areas.
- Incorporate best practices to ensure timely, accurate information and pay.
- Provide better service to military personnel and their families, including timely and accurate records of service and delivery of compensation, benefits, and entitlements.
- Create one record per service member that follows them across components and branches.
- Create one joint, personnel and pay system, providing standard data for comparison across services and components.
- Provide access to more-reliable and more-accurate personnel information for warfighter mission planning.
- Track all skill sets and help match members with appropriate assignments.
- Provide combatant commands (CoCOMs) an integrated view of assigned personnel.
- Subsume more than 80 legacy systems.

DIMHRS is based on a commercial off-the-shelf product, PeopleSoft™, and will be somewhat standardized across the Department of Defense. Air Force and Army subject-matter experts (SMEs) are redesigning processes and addressing data requirements to leverage PeopleSoft™ capabilities.

DIMHRS could bring more-significant changes because a key to automatically updating and sharing information is defining what data are available under specific circumstances and in what format. The specialty code is an illustrative example. PeopleSoftTM maintains job codes that are comparable to Air Force specialty codes, but the job-code field length is only six characters. This is not long enough to accommodate the five-digit enlisted AFSC plus a prefix and suffix. Job codes could become an even more complicated issue because, as discussed earlier, they are specific to each military service and their formats vary. The format for DIMHRS job codes could force changes to the structure of Air Force specialty codes.

The Changing Nature of Work

The changing nature of work is a far more subtle transformer that may eventually produce the most fundamental changes in the specialty-classification structure since 1954. Most developed countries are transitioning from industrial- to knowledge-based economies. While knowledge and information have always been important, the shift from the physicality of manufacturing to the preeminence of knowledge and information portends significant changes in occupations and the classification of occupations. *This shift is closely tied to the growing importance of technology and advanced processes, which are transforming the work that people perform and the methods used to accomplish that work.*

With the transition to a knowledge-based economy, many workers are being given a wider and higher-level scope of responsibilities, with increased decisionmaking authority (Landry, Mahesh, and Hartman, 2005). This trend is causing occupational boundaries to blur as the work becomes a more fluid combination of multiple task sets. Another trend is that work is

---

[14] For more discussion, see the Defense Integrated Military Human Resources System home page, n.d.

becoming more cognitively complex. Many tasks require increased analytic and judgmental skills to carry out work that is more novel, extemporaneous, and context-based, with few rules and structured ways of working. These analytic and judgmental skills often encompass the ability to think, learn, and solve problems that cut across occupational specialties.

Communication and information technologies have long been deeply intertwined into most aspects of work. However, technology breakthroughs—especially mobile technologies and the Internet—are enabling work to be separated with respect to time and space. This separation is prompting the rethinking of work and how and where it is performed.

The changing nature of both the work and the workers blurs the boundaries between who performs which jobs. Such blurring will have implications for most occupational classification systems, including the Air Force's. This is evinced in the changing lexicon and methods used for job analysis.[15] Although the definitions are still arguable, words such as competencies and competency modeling are in vogue. Increasingly, organizations are experimenting with competency frameworks and models to underpin their human resource strategies (Markus, Cooper-Thomas, and Allpress, 2005).

The Changing Nature of Warfare

Continual threats to national security, finite resources, the global war on terror, asymmetric warfare, frequent and multiple commitments across the globe, and complex interagency/multinational operations are the reality for America's military forces. As stated in the 2004 National Military Strategy (Joint Chiefs of Staff [JCS], 2004, p. 15), "Defeating adaptive adversaries requires flexible, modular and deployable joint forces with the ability to combine the strengths of individual services, combatant commands, other government agencies and multinational partners." This undoubtedly requires joint military capabilities, joint operating concepts, joint functional concepts, and critical enablers[16] adaptable to diverse conditions and objectives.

Every level of the national command structure calls for jointness as a means of maximizing force capabilities. The strategy outlined in the Capstone Concept for Joint Operations (JCS, 2005a, pp. 25–26) focuses on achieving military objectives while contributing to broader national objectives through unified action—i.e., integration with other agencies and multinational partners. Each service's vision statement and doctrine stress joint capabilities and effects-based joint operations. The 2006 Quadrennial Defense Review (QDR) (U.S. Department of Defense [DoD], 2006, p. 4) sought to accelerate "the transformation of the Department to focus more on the needs of Combatant Commanders and to develop portfolios of joint capabilities rather than individual stove-piped programs."

The 2006 QDR (DoD, p. 75) also stressed that the 21st century total force "must continue to adapt to different operating environments, develop new skills and rebalance its capabilities and people if it is to remain prepared for the new challenges of an uncertain future." Future warriors will be as proficient in irregular operations, including counterinsurgency and stabilization operations, as they are today in high-intensity combat. As one example, operations

---

[15] *Job analysis* was first used in the early 1900s by industrial engineers and efficiency experts looking for ways to save time, reduce errors, and increase productivity (Du Preez and Pintelon, 1997). Job analyses are conducted for compensation studies, training needs analysis, test validation, succession planning, job and organizational design, and other human resources activities.

[16] *Critical enablers* are capabilities considered crucial for joint operations to function as such and are essential to the accomplishment of the specified or assumed objective(s).

in Iraq and Afghanistan are blurring the division between basic soldiering and airman skills. The term *battlefield airman* readily designates specialties trained and poised to perform ground combat and bare-base operations in hostile territory, with its associated security challenges. However, battlefield airmen have also been on the ground with the Special Operations Forces (SOF) units from sister services. Also, specialized forces have been used in Army-like combat patrols, conducting raids and seizing suspected insurgents outside such facilities as Balad Air Base. In addition to battlefield airmen, airmen in other specialties conduct convoy and engineering missions "outside the perimeter" of an air base, which requires them to develop traditional Army skill sets.

The specialty-classification structure, like most infrastructure systems, is continually evolving through frequent local upgrades and improvements and infrequent global advancements. In this research effort, we sought to look beyond these current and planned changes to determine which other changes might be warranted. Those changes are discussed in the next chapter.

CHAPTER FOUR

Recommended Specialty-Structure Changes

As mentioned in Chapter One, the authors were members of an Air Force AFSC Reengineering Working Group. In an effort to provide a comprehensive analysis, we reached beyond ongoing and planned changes to identify areas that might have been overlooked. We conducted 18 interview sessions that included classification specialists from the Air Force and the other services, occupational measurement specialists, and selected career-field managers of large and small specialties groups. We analyzed observations gleaned from briefings given to the reengineering working group, as well as data from Air Force and Defense Manpower Data Center (DMDC) manpower and personnel data systems. This chapter presents our observations as they relate to the officer portion of the specialty-classification structure.

Comparisons with Other Services

The interviews, data analysis, and cross-sectional analysis of each service's classification structure highlighted several similarities and differences that reinforce current practices.[1]

Using Specialty, Subspecialty, and Additional Skills Codes to Match People and Jobs

Each service's specialty coding structures use a combination of numbers and/or letters to match people and jobs. The basic officer specialty codes for the Navy, Marine Corps, and Air Force have four digits. The basic Army officer specialty code has three digits. Here are some distinguishing features, by service.

Air Force. The Air Force officer specialty code contains four alphanumeric characters (DAF, 2006). The first two digits are numeric, the first identifying the career group (e.g., 1xxx is operations) and combining with the second to identify the utilization field[2] (e.g., 11xx is pilot; 12xx is navigator). The third, alphabetic, digit combines with the first two digits to identify the functional area (e.g., 11Bx is bomber pilot; 12Bx is bomber navigator). The fourth digit indicates the qualification level. This 4-digit AFSC may be augmented with an alphabetic prefix and/or suffix, resulting in a six-digit code. These codes may be supplemented with separate special-experience identifiers (SEIs) to identify unique experience or training.

1 The cross-sectional analysis was based on data collected during summer 2007.

2 A *utilization field* as depicted in Chapter Two is a group of Air Force officer specialties, related by required skills and knowledge. It may consist of only one specialty if the skills and knowledge required are unique and do not relate to other officer specialties.

Army. The Army area of concentration (AOC) contains three alphanumeric characters (Department of the Army [DA], 2005). The first two digits of the AOC are numeric and identify the branch or functional area (FA).[3] A *functional area* is a general skill set and is broader than the branches. Newly commissioned Army officers initially receive AOC and branch designations. After the fifth or sixth year of service, officers may receive an FA designation. As in the Air Force, the AOC may be supplemented by a skill identifier (SI), which indicates special schooling, training, and experiences. These identifiers are not related to any particular branch, FA, or career field.

Marine Corps. The U.S. Marine Corps (USMC) military occupational specialty contains four numeric digits (USMC, 2005). The first two digits identify the occupational field. The remaining two digits designate the specialty.

Navy. The Navy officer designator codes contain four numeric digits (DN, 2006). The fourth digit denotes whether the officer has a regular (0), Reserve (5), or full-time support (7) commission. Also, Navy officers have one or more three-character additional qualification designators (AQDs) that reflect completion of requirements qualifying them in a specific warfare area or other specialization. In a sense, AQDs function more like the AFSCs, AOCs, or MOSs in the other services than do the designators. To identify qualifications beyond the designator and AQDs, the Navy uses subspecialty (SSP) codes (DN, 2006, Part B).

Also, the Navy designators are partitioned by the type of officer: unrestricted line, restricted line, staff corps, and limited duty officer (LDO). *Unrestricted line* officers may aspire to the warfighting command elements of the Navy. They receive training in tactics, strategy, command and control, and actual combat and are considered unrestricted because they are authorized to command ships, aviation squadrons, and special operations units. *Restricted line* officers are concentrated in non–combat-related fields, such as engineering, maintenance, meteorology and oceanography, and intelligence. They are not given training that would enable them to command combat units. *Staff corps* officers are specialists in fields that are themselves professional careers, such as medicine, law, and civil engineering. *LDOs* are former enlisted members who are commissioned based on their skill and expertise, and they are not required to have a bachelor's degree.

Table 4.1 provides a comparative illustration of the services' officer specialty coding schema. In this example, the Air Force F-15 pilot is quickly identified at the subspecialty level by the suffix "F" added to the AFSC "11F3." The Army AH-64C/D pilot is not identified until the AOC "15A" is combined with skill code information, "D7" in this case. Such identification requires matching data from different data-code tables. The Marine Corps appears to have the most efficient method: The F/A-18 pilot is identified by the MOS "7521," the most information in the fewest digits. The Navy appears to have the most complicated structure. The Navy F/A-18 pilot with a regular commission is not identified until the designator "1310" is combined with ACDs "DA7," "DB6," or "DCF." This table suggests the *Air Force has one of the more efficient structures for identifying specific competencies.*

---

[3] An *Army branch* is a grouping of officers that makes up an arm or service of the Army in which an officer is commissioned or transferred, trained, developed, and promoted. All officers hold a single branch designation and may serve repetitive and progressive assignments associated with that branch. An *Army functional area* is an interrelated grouping of tasks or skills that usually require significant education, training, and experience, possessed by officers who are grouped by career field rather than arm, service, or branch.

Table 4.1
Examples of Services' Specialty Codings for Active Duty Pilots

	Service (Aircraft)							
	Air Force (F-15)		Army (AH-64)		Marine Corps (F/A-18)		Navy (F/A-18)	
Utilization field, branch, community	11	Pilot	15	Aviation	75	Pilot/NFO	13	URL Pilot/NFO
Specialty, AOC, designator	11F	Fighter Pilot	15A	Aviation, General	7521	F-18 Pilot	1310	URL Pilot
Subspecialty	11F3F	F-15 Fighter Pilot						
Special experience identifier, additional skill identifier, skill code			D7	AH-64C/D Pilot			DA7, DB6, or DCF	FA-18 light attack, FA-18 fighter/bomber, FAC

Commonality Between Officer and Enlisted Occupational Groupings

One of the principles for the Air Force 1993 specialty restructuring was to align officer and enlisted AFSCs by mirroring the first characters in both (Boles, 1993). It was believed this would help align personnel and maintain functional integrity. The degree of alignment between the officer and enlisted specialty codes varies among the services.

Air Force. The first digit of both the officer and enlisted AFSCs is numeric, and in both cases it designates the career group (DAF, 2006): operations (1), logistics (2), support (3), medical (4), legal or chaplain (5), acquisition or finance (6), special investigation (7), special-duty identifier (8), and reporting identifier (9). The direct linkage ends here. The second digit for an officer is a numeric character, which, when combined with the first digit, designates the *utilization field.* For example, the first two digits of a fighter pilot's AFSC "11F3" denote the utilization field for pilots. The second digit for enlisted personnel is alphabetic and, when combined with the first digit, designates the *career field.* For example, the first two digits of an aircraft load master's AFSC "1A271" denote the utilization field for aircrew operations.

Army. The first two digits of the commissioned officer AOC and the warrant officer and enlisted personnel MOSC are numeric (DA, 1997; DA, 2007a; DA, 2005). For commissioned and warrant officers, these two digits designate the branch or functional area. For enlisted personnel, the two digits usually designate the career-management field, which is comparable to enlisted career fields in the Air Force. The two-digit clusters share the same occupational titles in both officer and enlisted classification structures. The linkage ends at this point. The third digit for commissioned officers is an alphabetic character and completes the AOC. As an example, the AOC for air defense artillery officer is "14A."

For warrant officers, the third digit is a number. The warrant officer MOSC is similar to those for enlisted personnel, except that the first three digits are numeric and the MOSC does not contain a skill level identifier. An example is the Patriot systems technician seven-digit MOSC "140ET2B" "140" warrant officer in the air defense artillery branch. The nine-digit MOSC for a sergeant first class who is a Patriot fire control enhanced operator/maintainer could be "14E4OYYZZ," depending on special qualifications, additional skills, and foreign-language proficiency. The third digit of the enlisted MOSC is alphabetic (an "E" in this case) and is used to designate the specific specialty. The fourth digit of the enlisted MOS represents skill level, which is commensurate with rank and grade.[4]

Marine Corps. The military occupational specialties for all Marines—commissioned officers, warrant officers, enlisted personnel—are the four-digit numeric codes described earlier (USMC, 2005). For commissioned and warrant officers, the last two digits designate the specialty. As examples, MOS "0803" designates a field artillery officer, whereas "0840" designates a naval fire support planner. For enlisted personnel, the last two digits identify the promotional channel[5] and specialty. As examples, the enlisted MOS "0811" denotes a field artillery cannoneer (master gunnery sergeant to private) and "0842" denotes a field artillery radar operator (sergeant to private). In each of these examples, the first two digits "08" designate the occupational field as *field artillery*.

Navy. The Navy divides its specialties into *designators* for officers and *ratings* for enlisted personnel. No commonality exists between the two structures. The officer designators were described earlier. The Navy Enlisted Occupational Classification System consists of the enlisted-rating structure and its supplement, the Navy Enlisted Classification (NEC) structure. The enlisted-rating structure combines the specialty and the rank into two- to four-digit abbreviations. The specialty portion has two alphabetic characters based on the title of the rating. For example, an electrician technician third class (pay grade E-4) would have the rating "ET3." A senior chief petty officer electrician (pay grade E-8) would have the rating "ETCS." The NEC structure supplements the rating structure by identifying nonrating-wide skills/knowledge/aptitudes/qualifications that must be documented to appropriately identify both people and billets. The identifier is a four-digit code that captures skills and abilities beyond those that are standard for the particular rating. As examples, "ET-1402" would indicate an electrician with advanced training in tactical communications maintenance, and "ET-1407," an electrician with advanced training in shipboard air traffic control communications.

Each service's human capital system is geared to its particular military specialty-classification structure. The differences within each service and across the services are indicative of the challenges that must be overcome before a common manpower and personnel system, such as DIMHRS, can be implemented DoD-wide.

Mission-Driven Specialty Differences

In even the most complex organization, there is a set of people with knowledge, skills, and orientations that are nearly identical to the mission and activities of the organization, and they become the core elite of their organization (Mosher, 1982, pp. 122–123). As would be expected, the services' officer specialty structures depict some specialties with clear linkages to their primary missions.

Air Force. The Air Force's Operations career group is composed of pilots, navigators, and space, missiles, command and control (C2) specialists. There are ten functional areas for pilots, nine for navigators, and five for space, missile, and C2 specialists. Pilots are classified as: bomber (11B), test (11E), fighter (11F), generalist (11G), helicopter (11H), trainer (11K),

---

[4] The basic enlisted MOSC is the first five-digits: MOS, skill level, and special qualification. However, personnel requisitions use the nine-digit MOSC, which adds the ASI (additional skill identifiers) as the sixth and seventh characters and foreign-language qualifications as the eighth and ninth characters.

[5] Each job has authorized ranks. For example, anyone ranking from private to sergeant can be a rifleman (0311), but only Marines ranking from staff sergeant to master gunnery sergeant can be an infantry unit leader (0369).

mobility (11M), reconnaissance/surveillance/electronic warfare (11R), special operations (11S), and remotely operated aircraft (11U). Navigators are classified in a similar manner, except that there are no navigators for helicopters. The space, missile, and C2 specialties divide as follows: astronaut (13A), air battle manager (13B), control and recovery (13D), airfield operations (13M), and space and missiles (13S). Excluding the Medical group, the Operations group has the largest delineation of officer specialties. Most of the other utilization fields correspond to one functional area.

Army. Army commanders use maneuver, fires, and other elements of combat power to defeat or destroy enemy forces. Infantry, aviation, and armor are closely linked to maneuver. Field artillery and air defense artillery are closely linked to fires. The Army's combat arms group is composed of seven branches. Only one AOC, "A," is associated with six of these branches—infantry (10A), field artillery (13A), air defense artillery (14A), aviation (15A), Special Forces (18A), and Corps of Engineers (21A)—whereas the armor branch has three AOCs: armor general (19A), armor (19B), and cavalry (19C).

Marine Corps. The Marine Corps ground combat MOSs are infantry (0302), field artillery (0802), tank (1802), and combat engineer (1302). Marine Corps pilots make up the "75xx" occupational field. Similarly to the Air Force, several MOSs within this occupational field are used to designate specific types of pilots.

Navy. The Navy's unrestricted line officer designators are surface warfare (111x), submarine warfare (112x), special warfare—UDT (underwater demolition team) SEALs (113x), Special Operations–divers and EOD (114x), pilot (131x), and naval flight officer (132x). Officers with these designators may become eligible for command of ships, submarines, aircraft squadrons, fleets, and shore installations.

People in the specialties cited above are most closely associated with their respective service's core missions. According to Mosher's research, people in these specialties will define the mission and decide on the capabilities needed to carry it out. This argues that the *services would want to preserve in their classification structure the ability to precisely track, train, and develop their core elites.*

Mission-Driven Differences in Logistics Specialties

According to JCS Pub 1-02, *logistics* is the science of planning and carrying out the movement and maintenance of forces (JCS, 2005a, p. 317). At the operational and tactical levels, *logistics* may be thought of as moving, supplying, and maintaining military forces. It is basic to the ability of armies, fleets, and air forces to operate. Table 4.2 shows the logistics officer specialties by service. The Air Force has the fewest specialties, which is not surprising, given the other services' diversity of weapon systems and relative amount of large-scale troop and equipment movements.

Table 4.3 shows that, excluding civil engineering, the services have comparable levels of granularity among the support specialties. As discussed in Chapter Three, the Air Force is planning to eliminate the subspecialties in civil engineering, a change that would make it equivalent to the other services.

Table 4.2
Comparison of Logistics Officer Specialties

Air Force	Army	Marine Corps	Navy
	Aviation, Ship and Submarine Maintenance		
21A Aircraft Maintenance	15D Aviation Logistics	6002 Aircraft Maintenance	144X RL (Engineering Duty Officer)
		5902 LDO (Aviation Electronic Maintenance)	152X RL (Aviation Maintenance)
			613X LDO (Engineering/ Repair—Surface)
			623X LDO (Engineering/ Repair—Submarine)
			633X LDO (Aviation Maintenance)
	Ordnance, Munition, and Missile Maintenance		
21M Munitions and Missile Maintenance	89E Explosive Ordnance Disposal	Only Warrant Officers	616X LDO (Ordnance—surface)
Subspecialty 21MxC: Nuclear	91A Maintenance and Munitions	Only Warrant Officers	626X LDO (Ordnance—submarine)
			636X LDO (Ordnance—aviation)
			648X LDO (EOD)
	Readiness, Transportation, Supply		
21R Logistics Readiness	90A Logistics	0402 Logistics	310X Staff Corps (Supply Corps)
	88A Transportation—General	3002 Ground Supply	6510 LDO (Supply Corps)
	88B Traffic Management	3502 Motor Transport	*Subspecialties* 1301: Supply Acquisition, Distribution 1302: Systems Inventory Management 1304: Transportation Logistics Management 1305: Retailing 1306: Acquisition and Contract Management 1307: Petroleum Management
	88C Marine and Terminal Operations	6602 Aviation Supply	
	88D Motor/Rail		
	92A Quartermaster—General		
	92D Aerial Delivery and Material		
	92F Petroleum and Water		

NOTES: This table does not include warrant officer specialties. Also, there are no subspecialties unless shown.

Ideas for Change

The interviews, data analysis, and cross-service analysis also revealed changes the Air Force should consider.

Table 4.3
Comparison of Services' Support Officer Specialties

Air Force	Army	Marine Corps	Navy
	Security Forces, Military Police		
31P Security Forces	31A Military Police	5803 Military Police	649X LDO (Security)
	Civil Engineer; Combat Engineer; Facilities, Contract/Construction Management Engineer (FCCME)		
32E Civil Engineer	21A Engineer-General	1302 Engineer	510X Staff Corps (Civil Engineer Corps)
Subspecialties (suffixes) 32ExA: Architect 32ExB: Readiness 32ExC: Civil Engineer 32ExD: Readiness (Non-Engineer) 32ExE: Electrical Engineer 32ExF: Mechanical Engineer 32ExG: General Engineer 32ExH: EOD Engineer 32ExJ: Environmental Engineer 32ExK: EOD (Non-Engineer)	21B Combat Engineer 21D Facilities/Construction		653X LDO (Civil Engineer Corps) *Subspecialties* 1101: Facilities Engineering 1103: Ocean Engineering
	Communication & Information, Signal, Info Systems		
33C Communications Commander	25A Signal—General	0602 Comm Info Systems	629X LDO (Comm—submarine)
33S Communications and Information	24A Open Systems Engineer	2502 Communication	642X LDO (Info systems)
Subspecialties (suffixes) 33SxA: Comm & Info Engineer	24X Info Systems Engineer 53A Info Systems Management	4002 Data Systems	169X SDO (Merchant Marine—comm)
	Manpower-Personnel, Human Resources, Adjutant		
37F Manpower-Personnel	42B Human Resources	0180 Adjutant	120X SDO (Human Resources)
Subspecialties (suffixes) 37FxQ: Squadron Section Commander	42H Senior Human Resources		*Subspecialties* 3130: Manpower Systems Analysis 3150: Education and Training

NOTES: This table does not include warrant officer specialties. Also, there are no subspecialties unless shown.

More Granularity Among Intelligence Specialties

Intelligence is a function that is common to all of the services. Table 4.4 shows that there were 10,839 active duty intelligence officers among the four military services, and that the Air Force had the second-largest total. Of DoD's active duty intelligence officers, 28 percent are Air Force members. Yet, as the table shows, the Air Force has the least differentiation among officer

Table 4.4
Active Duty Intelligence Officer Specialties, by Service

	Air Force		Army		Marine Corps		Navy	
Active Duty Intelligence Officers	3,087		4,239		1,377		2,136	
Utilization field, branch, community	14	Intelligence	35	Intelligence	02	Intelligence	163	Intelligence
Specialty, AOC, MOS, designator	14N	Intelligence	35C	Imagery	0201	Basic Intelligence	1610	Cryptologic (Restricted Line)
			35D	All source	0202	MAGTF	1630	Intelligence (Restricted Line)
			35E	Counter Intelligence	0203	Ground	6450	Intelligence (LDO)
			35F	Human	0204	Human		
			35G	Signals/EW	0206	Signal/ Ground EW		
			34A	Strategic Intelligence	0207	Air		
Subspecialties							2200	Regional, general
							2201	Middle East, Africa, South Asia
							2202	Far East/Pacific
							2203	Western Hemisphere
							2204	Europe, Russia
							2400	Strategic

SOURCE: Data extract from Defense Manpower Data Center, 2007.

intelligence specialties. JCS Pub 1-02 (2005b, p. 268) lists more than 40 intelligence activities, which argues for the need for greater differentiation.[6]

Table 4.5 shows that Air Force intelligence officers are assigned to a wide array of organizations with diverse missions, which suggests that the officers may be involved in activities related to air superiority, close air support, interdiction, special operations, mobility, ground support, force protection, search and rescue, and battle damage assessment. Some officers serve in joint intelligence operations centers supporting joint and combined forces. Intelligence officers may work with products derived from satellites, U-2s, airborne warning and control systems, RC-135s, unmanned aerial vehicles (UAVs) (such as the Predator and Global Hawk), as well as many other systems. The officers may work with and lead enlisted personnel with specialties in intelligence applications, imagery, communication signals, electronic signals, network intelligence, and cryptology. This, a priori, argues that greater differentiation may be warranted.

[6] Examples include acoustic intelligence, all-source intelligence, basic intelligence, combat intelligence, communications intelligence, electronic intelligence, electro-optical intelligence, foreign intelligence, signals intelligence, human intelligence, imagery intelligence, joint intelligence, laser intelligence, nuclear intelligence, open-source intelligence, operational intelligence, photographic intelligence, strategic intelligence, tactical intelligence, target intelligence, and technical intelligence.

Table 4.5
Intelligence Officers, by Organization Type

Organizations	Number of Officers
USAF squadrons, wings, headquarters	1,917
Unified commands	432
USAF agencies (AIA, Analysis, T&E, Tech App)	459
DoD agencies (DIA, DTRA, Geospatial)	241
Others	38
Total	3,087

NOTES: AIA = Air Intelligence Agency; T&E = AF Operational Test and Evaluation Center; Tech App = AF Technical Application Center; DIA = Defense Intelligence Agency; DTRA = Defense Threat Reduction Agency.

One objective of a specialty-classification structure is to inform the rest of the human capital system about the qualifications needed and when they are needed. Without these parameters, the system cannot adequately gauge the preparation and development of its workforce. The current Air Force specialty-classification structure would suggest, depending on rank, that a generic "14N" fits all situations. Given the diversity of jobs, having such a catch-all categorization could easily lead to underpreparation or overpreparation of Air Force intelligence officers.

In 2006, the Air Force started redrawing the intelligence organizational boxes to provide the necessary flexibility for moving new capabilities to the warfighter as conditions change and technologies improve (Ackerman, 2007). Our comparison with other services suggests that the Air Force should also consider increasing the granularity within the intelligence specialty to better calibrate its training and development programs. The Army and Marine Corps use multiple specialties. The Navy uses multiple subspecialties. The Air Force's increased granularity should be balanced with the need for career-field sustainability and appropriate officer growth and development.

Embedding the Qualification Level in the Specialty Code

Recall that, in the elements of the Air Force officer four-digit AFSC, the fourth digit indicates the qualification level. The qualification levels are qualified commander (0), entry (1), intermediate (2) (used only for pilots, bomber navigators, and missile launch officers), qualified (3), and staff (4), which denotes level of functional responsibility and is restricted to above wing level.

The services, universally, embed skill or qualification levels into the specialty-coding structure for their enlisted ranks. The Army uses the fourth digit of the nine-digit enlisted MOS. The skill level correlates to the rank and grade. The Marine Corps controls the entry into specialties based on rank. The underlying principle is that increased duties and tasks accompany promotions. The Navy adds numeric or alphabetic digits corresponding to pay grade to the ratings.

By contrast, the inclusion of qualification levels in the specialty code for officers is peculiar to the Air Force. Table 4.6 summarizes the qualification codes shown in the Manpower Programming and Execution System (MPES) for fiscal year 2008, as of December 2007. MPES does not normally use the entry-level qualification code; however, this code is useful

Table 4.6
Officer Qualification Codes Used in MPES, by Organization Level

	Required Qualification Level				
Organizational Level	**0**	**2**	**3**	**4**	**Total**
Hq USAF	124		26	1,495	1,645
Joint (Multi-Service)	221		1,090	4,649	5,960
MAJCOM Hq	141		100	2,589	2,830
NAF Hq/AU	1,165		447	672	2,284
Center	125		1,104	418	1,647
FOA/DRU	293		1,539	1,608	3,440
Wing/Group/Squadron	1,330	1,854	32,957	390	36,531
Other	110		1,762	1,148	3,020
Unknown	13		315	14	342
Grand Total	3,522	1,854	39,340	12,983	57,699

in the personnel data system to help track training progression and monitor the health of the workforce.

All of the intermediate-level positions were in operational squadrons, and nearly 80 percent of those positions were for lieutenants. Over 90 percent of all officer positions require a fully qualified or staff officer.

The question is whether level 4 provides additional information or is an unnecessary redundancy. As expected, the overwhelming majority of field-grade positions at Headquarters USAF and the MAJCOM headquarters had 4 as the required qualification level. This is easily identified because the organization level is specified in the manpower documents in the organization-type column. Sometimes, as Table 4.6 suggests, the level-4 code is used improperly. For example, 390 positions at wing level or below had this qualification level, which is contrary to the guidance for its use. It appears that the use of qualification level 4 merely duplicates what is otherwise revealed by the organizational level and grade of the positions; it may even result in inaccurate information.

Creating More "Any Officer" Jobs

The other services' classification structures more explicitly recognize that many jobs may be filled by personnel from any of several specialties. These are not the jobs for which the Air Force would use SDIs or RIs. Table 4.7 shows the set of codes that are variants of "any officer."

Previous research strongly suggests that the Air Force has many jobs that could be filled by variants of the "any officer" designation (Moore, Thomas, and Conley, 2007). Table 4.8 presents an extract of the data collected from MPES to determine what type of occupational-skill pairings were needed among Air Force colonels. The data show that, of the 2,778 jobs included in the study, 40 percent were variants of "any officer." By extrapolation based on the types of jobs, we believe that more "any officer" jobs exist in the other grades. Creating and using "any officer" codes to identify jobs that could be filled by people from a variety of specialties would increase the accuracy of stated requirements, reduce artificial specificity, and allow greater latitude in assigning officers to jobs. However, doing so will require developing a methodol-

Table 4.7
Codes for Jobs That May Be Filled by "Any Officer"

Air Force		Army		Marine Corps		Navy	
Code	**Title**	**Code**	**Title**	**Code**	**Title**	**Code**	**Title**
11G	Generalist Pilot	01A	Any officer—officer generalist	9965	Any fixed-wing pilot	1000	Any URL or SD officer
12G	Generalist Navigator	01B	Aviation/infantry/ armor/military intelligence	9966	Any naval flight officer	1020	Any URL or SD (Info Professional)
		02A	Combat arms	9967	Any helicopter pilot	1050	Any URL (Warfare specialties)
		02B	Infantry/armor	9969	Any pilot or NFO	1302	Any URL (Pilot or NFO)
		02C	Infantry/armor/field artillery/engineer				
		03A	Infantry/armor				
		05A	Army medical—any medical				

NOTES: NFO = Naval Flight Officer; URL = Unrestricted Line; SD = special duty.

Table 4.8
Colonel Positions Requiring Variant of "Any Officer"

Job Requirement	Colonel Positions
Any Line Officer	548
Any Rated	267
Any Acquisition	133
Any Fighter or Bomber Pilot/Navigator	59
Any Fighter/Bomber/Airlift Pilot/Navigator	42
Any Rated, excluding ABM (13B)	36
Total	1,085

NOTES: These data were collected in 2002 and have not been updated. They are used here merely to illustrate that the Air Force has a large number of jobs that could be more accurately coded as a variant of "any officer" than the more-specific specialties shown in MPES. ABM = Air Battle Manager.

ogy for assigning these positions to accessionable AFSCs to grow and develop officers for these billets.

Requirements for Multiple Specialties

Earlier research established that many senior-officer positions should be filled by people qualified in more than one specialty—a primary and a secondary (Robbert et al., 2005; Moore, Thomas, and Conley, 2007). A review of personnel requisitions replicated those findings and indicated that many other field-grade jobs may require qualifications in multiple specialties. Interviews with career-field managers, development team leaders, and assignment managers suggested a major hurdle in getting functional communities to develop people with appropriate primary and secondary specialties.

The major hurdle is that the *multispecialty requirements are not visible in the MPES or the UMDs.* A few development teams have provided officers' developmental assignments in secondary specialties based on survey data and various models (Moore, Thomas, and Conley, 2007, pp. 3–5, 89), but they considered these Excel-based methods inadequate for effective force management. Assignment managers typically rely on personnel requisitions from the hiring authority to identify jobs requiring experience in more than one specialty. The requisition forms arrive as jobs become eligible for fill—one job at a time—and do not provide a picture of the total requirements. *No systematic method exists to aggregate, evaluate, and plan for multispecialty requirements.* Most interviewees opined that this part of force development would be dysfunctional until multispecialty requirements, wherever they might exist, are given visibility in the manpower data system.

The Navy and Army offer two contrasting ways to handle multispecialty requirements. Navy subspecialty codes, integral components of its manpower and personnel classification control system, are used to identify secondary requirements and qualifications (DN, 2006, Part B). The required area of specialization (specialty) for a particular billet is identified by the applicable designator code. The subspecialty codes specify a major field of application and area of concentration. For example, a billet might require a surface warfare officer (designator: 1110) with a subspecialty in strategic intelligence (SSP: 2400). Navy unit manpower documents reflect designator and subspecialty codes for each billet.

The Army routinely develops officers with multispecialties through functional-area assignments. A few FA examples are strategic intelligence (FA34), human resources (FA43), foreign area officer (FA48), and strategic plans and policy (FA59). Under the Officer Personnel Management System (OPMS), lieutenants are accessed into the Army's basic branches. Their basic branch becomes their basic specialty. About midway through the company grade years, officers have the opportunity to select and be designated in an FA (DA, 2005, pp. 14, 53). Initial FA assignments usually occur after officers complete their captain-level branch-development requirements.

For example, depending on education and experience, an infantry officer (AOC: 11A) could receive a human resource management (FA: 43) or space operations (FA: 30) assignment. Later, immediately following selection to major, officers are designated into a branch or FA by a centralized career-selection board. Some officers retain the FA specialty and enter operational support, institutional support, or information operations career fields. Others retain their basic branch affiliation and enter the operations career field.

Unlike in the Navy, Air Force multispecialty requirements are not documented in its unit manpower documents. Unlike in the Army, the Air Force does not produce a cohort of multispecialty officers. Several interviewees suggested that *adding one column to the UMD for a secondary specialty would increase the visibility of its multispecialty requirements.* Increasing the visibility of these requirements should provide a more complete description of job requirements and, through the *normal refinement processes*—periodic updates to the manpower document—improve their accuracy. The development teams and assignment managers could more clearly understand how officers would be developed for and utilized in these jobs.

More Agility

All interviewees—classification specialists, assignment managers, career-field managers—insisted that the process for making changes to the specialties codes and content should maintain or even increase the process's rigor. Modifications to the specialty codes, the content, and their structure have significant effects on all facets of human capital management. Accordingly, the process should ensure that specialty changes are justified and prudent.

While seeing the need to preserve due diligence, the interviewees also insisted the processes for making changes need reengineering to reduce the amount of time required and increase the responsiveness of the system. Communication-computer and logistics career-field managers indicated that, 20 years ago, it could take a decade or more for technology to fundamentally change specialty content and spark adjustments. Then, a two- or three-year cycle to make changes to AFSCs may have been acceptable. In today's more rapidly changing environment, even 12 to 18 months is not responsive enough.

More Rigor in SEI Codes

Several interviewees described the system for SEI codes as "undisciplined." As discussed in Chapter Two, more than 7,200 separate officer SEIs are possible. However, fewer than 600 officer SEI codes are actively used in the MPES and, as shown in Table 4.9, less than 4 percent of all officer positions have SEI codes. The largest numbers of SEI-coded positions were found in developmental engineering, acquisition management, intelligence, air battle management, and security forces. Airfield operations, security forces, air battle management, and developmental engineers were the only relatively large communities for which more than 10 percent of the positions had an SEI code. Developmental engineering, acquisition, scientist, and intelligence used the largest number of different SEI codes.

Several functional-community managers (e.g., Civil Engineering, Medical, Personnel/Manpower/Services) suggested that there is a policy void relating to the use of suffixes as opposed to SEI codes. Indeed, our review of the use of SEI codes in the manpower data system indicated that some functional communities (e.g., Intelligence, Developmental Engineering) could be using SEI codes as surrogates for suffixes or to work around the specialty-classification codes. We observed that several SEI codes (e.g., YTR—targeting, YZT—tactical intelligence) had relatively high use, but within one specialty (14N—intelligence). As a more specific example, the code OCE (Air Surveillance Officer) was used 105 times—all within the air battle manager specialty (13B).

As a contrast, we observed that several SEI codes had relatively high use and were distributed across several specialties. For example, SEI code 9AY (Air Operations Center) was used 226 times among 22 specialties, and SEI code OB6 (Flight Commander) was used 100 times among five bomber and mobility specialties. Furthermore, because several thousand codes exist with no edits[7] by AFSC,[8] there is limited oversight of officer SEIs in the manpower data system. Edits by AFSC do exist for the enlisted specialties. However, classification specialists and enlisted career-field managers indicated that the accuracy and rigor of those SEIs varied by functional community.

Although the assignment directive (DAF, 2005, p. 30) references SEIs, there are no established procedures for using them in the officer-assignment process. Normally, it is the individual officer's responsibility to request award or withdrawal of SEI codes. Yet, from the person (as opposed to job) side of the equation, SEIs have at times been viewed as undesirable because,

---

7 These data edits would enable detection and correction of major inconsistencies at the point of data entry.

8 *Edits* reflect the relationship between the AFSC and the SEI code.

Table 4.9
Summary of Special-Experience Identifier (SEI) Usage in Manpower Requirements Data System

Specialty	AFS	Total Positions	SEI-Coded Positions	Percentage SEI Coded	# SEI Codes Used
Developmental Engineer	62E	2,629	288	11.0	96
Acquisition Manager	63A	2,618	226	8.6	64
Scientist	61S	879	45	5.1	32
Intelligence	14N	2,578	163	6.3	31
Contracting	64P	705	35	5.0	20
Logistics Readiness	21R	1,590	71	4.5	17
Aircraft Maintenance	21A	1,438	62	4.3	10
Cost Analysis	65W	111	16	14.4	10
Mobility Navigator	12M	765	27	3.5	9
Bomber Navigator	12B	818	39	4.8	8
Security Forces	31P	684	130	19.0	7
Program Director	60C	61	8	13.1	7
Air Battle Manager	13B	1,270	162	12.8	6
Bomber Pilot	11B	694	30	4.3	6
Test Pilot	11E	140	14	10.0	5
Airfield Operations	13M	305	60	19.7	4
Dentist	47G	728	30	4.1	4
Special Operations Navigator	12S	490	20	4.1	3
Logistics Commander	20C	183	7	3.8	3
All Others		43,298	596	1.4	230
Total		61,984	2,029	3.3	572

SOURCE: Extract from Manpower Programming and Execution System (MPES), as of June 2006.

once awarded and coded in the manpower and personnel systems, they can be perceived as detrimental by individual airmen. Unless an Air Force member wishes to become a specialist in an occupational or technological subspecialty, he or she might avoid SEI qualification and recognition.

Lastly, because the current SEI system lacks rigor, consideration needs to be given to the temporal value of SEIs: What is their shelf life in a fast-changing environment? Can they be used accurately to identify special experiences?

Specialty-Classification Tenets

The specialty-classification concepts and tenets are supposed to be fundamental principles shared by those closely involved with the classification structure. Most of the career-field managers we interviewed were aware of the fundamental concepts: functional grouping and practical specialization. However, very few were aware of the tenets. The classification specialists referred to the tenets not as fundamental principles but, rather, as a checklist to be followed in developing changes to the classification structure. Recall from Chapter Two that the current classification tenets relate to purpose, grouping guidelines, criteria, and administration.

The question becomes: Is this list of tenets appropriately guiding specialty classification in an era of human capital management instead of industrial-age human resource management? Are there more-relevant tenets in today's technology-driven information era, with its emphasis on agility, flat organizations, problem-solving, networking, and distributed decisionmaking? We offer the following tenets for consideration:

- **Conserve Human Capital.** *Human capital* can be defined as productive capacity gained through investments[9] in education, training, experience, or other forms of development (Becker, 1983). Organizations are not only defining their human capital, but, increasingly, they are seeking to measure and optimize their human capital (Weatherly, 2003).[10] The combination of general and organization-specific training and learning should increase the employee's productivity and value to the organization (Swanson, 2001, pp. 109–114). To optimize investments in human capital, specialties should encompass a range of duties that is compact enough to allow initial skills training to a reasonable depth within a reasonable course length, and such that experience gained in earlier jobs is reasonably well reapplied in increasing productivity in later jobs. Conserving human capital can be achieved through three subtenets:
  - ***Create Functional Groups.*** As discussed in Chapter Two, work requirements and their corresponding specialties should be clustered into relatively homogeneous groups. The criteria are currently based on the amount of task and KSA commonality and complementariness. Although the variables for comparison might change under an alternative paradigm, such as competency-based job analysis (i.e., whether the system is based on KSAs or competencies, the functional groups should be based on commonality and complementariness), the concept of clustering into relatively homogeneous groups would still be fundamental.
  - ***Use Practical Specialization When Advantageous.*** Also as discussed in Chapter Two, practical specialization recognizes that no one person is likely to perform all of a specialty's tasks in any one job. However, given the specialty's minimum and desired qualifications, airmen should be able to perform all duties and responsibilities of the various jobs encountered throughout their careers with the least amount of additional training. When practical specialization is feasible, do not subdivide the specialty any further.
  - ***Create New Suffix or Specialty When Practical Specialization Is Not Advantageous.*** When practical specialization is infeasible, the existing or proposed aggregation should be further subdivided to create a separate suffix or specialty. From a human-capital perspective, the question becomes "*Does additional specialization improve productivity and increase the return on the investment for training or education?*"

[9] *Investments* include direct costs of training, education and experience, and indirect costs such as employee salary paid while being trained, salary of other employees who provide the training, and loss of productivity during adjustment periods.

[10] For example, the Chief Human Capital Officer (CHCO) Act of 2002 requires major federal agencies to have human capital executive positions and develop and track measures of human capital.

If the answer is yes, this tenet would encourage a subdivision of the specialty. If the answer is no, this tenet would discourage further subdivision.

- **Ensure That Specialties Are Sustainable or Manageable.** The specialty structure should provide *a framework that aids accessing into, training, and developing a sustainable, broadly experienced force.* Thus, a career field's skill and grade structure should be sustainable on its own or in combination with others. When a career field is not sustainable, a plan should exist for it to feed into or draw from other career fields as appropriate.
- **Preserve Career Viability.** The classification structure should provide *visible career paths*, offering sequential and progressive assignments benefiting the Air Force and the officers (DAF, 2006, p. 6). It should support other facets of the human capital system, such as appropriate force development and equity in promotion opportunities. For example, one principle of force development is that institutional competencies are developed by rotations (assignments) through multiple environments. If a specialty is defined too narrowly, the opportunities for assignments in multiple environments may be limited and restrict the development of institutional competencies.

The utility of these tenets was demonstrated in conjunction with two recent specialty restructures. The tenets were used to assist the Air Force in developing proposals for the classification structure for its emerging cyber-warrior specialties. Also, they were used to provide an assessment of potential issues resulting from the merger of Manpower, Personnel, and Services officer specialties. The tenets should continue being tested and refined in similar efforts.

Summary

Collectively, the insights gained from the interviews, data analysis, and cross-service analysis suggest that the Air Force system—a large and somewhat complicated system—is generally healthy but needs a few adjustments. The Air Force specialty-classification structure provides a framework that is robust and that has the appropriate inventory of functional job categories. Likewise, the classification framework is comprehensive and reflects the structure of the current workforce. The structure is comparable to its predecessors, permitting analyses of long-term trends in the characteristics of the workforce. The structure is transparent and readily understood by Manpower, Personnel, and Training managers. The shortcomings relate to granularity in at least one functional area, artificial specificity in some cases, insufficient rigor among SEI codes, and sluggishness when it comes to making changes.

The next chapter offers our conclusions and recommendations.

CHAPTER FIVE

Conclusions and Recommendations

Our review of major changes, work with the AFSC Reengineering Working Group, and analysis of ongoing and planned changes led to a finding that any major changes in the natural cluster of officer specialties would require the Air Force to rethink the role and uses of its officers. Therefore, only the mergers and consolidations noted by the working group should be tracked and implemented.[1] Coupling those analyses with the additional interviews, cross-service comparisons, and manpower and personnel data analyses discussed in Chapter Four, we derived the following conclusions and recommendations.

Conclusions

The Air Force specialty-classification structure is fundamentally sound, and, given its current use and operating environment, major modifications are not required. Since its inception 55 years ago, the structure has had only one major overhaul. It has proven to be robust and resilient. Given the ongoing and planned changes, restructurings on a par with those of 1993 are not needed currently.

As with any large, complex infrastructure, the specialty-classification components need continuous maintenance and periodic upgrades. Several upgrades are needed to address the following issues:

- There is no trigger mechanism that initiates and orchestrates an integrated response in specialty-related human capital activities when significant changes in missions, manpower, technology, and/or processes are planned. The Air Force launched an AFSO21 initiative to address this problem.
- Classification changes require cycle times that often take years to execute.
- The specialty-classification tenets are not functioning as guiding principles. Also, given the transition from industrial-age resource management to information-era human capital principles, the tenets need revision.
- Many jobs, particularly senior-officer jobs, require proficiency in a primary specialty and in a secondary specialty. The secondary requirements are not given visibility in the manpower data system. As a consequence, no systematic method exists to accurately aggregate, evaluate, and plan for multispecialty requirements.

[1] See pp. 15–16. The AFSC reengineering group's findings were briefed to the Air Force senior leadership in October 2007.

- The SEI code system for officers appears undisciplined: Thousands of such codes exist and are not linked to specific officer AFSCs, so there is limited oversight of officer SEIs in the manpower data system. This inability to associate and, if appropriate, restrict SEIs to specific officer AFSCs has led functional communities to consider and/or develop alternative systems to track special experiences.
- When compared with other services, the Air Force Intelligence specialty appears to lack sufficient granularity. Given the diversity of intelligence activities and the range of intelligence organizations, the Air Force should consider additional suffixes or more-rigorous use of SEI codes.
- Among the military services, the Air Force has the fewest variants of "any officer" codes. Because many jobs may be filled by officers from several specialties, identifying these requirements with a specific specialty results in artificial specificity and narrower utilization of officers.
- The Air Force is the only service that embeds the qualification level into the officer specialty code. A sample of the manpower data in MPES suggests that the qualification codes are useful; however, qualification code 4 duplicates information readily known from other data elements.

Major changes are occurring in the Air Force, DoD, the nature of work, and the nature of modern warfare. They will lead to significant changes in the specialty-classification structure. The Air Force is starting to populate its cyber activities. The creation of cyber-warriors will create changes in the specialty codes akin to those associated with the creation of specialties for the space missions. However, the migration to DIMHRS will produce the next major wholesale change to the specialty structure. Conceivably, the changing nature of work and warfare could lead to even more significant changes in the specialty structure.

Lastly, we think our findings have correlates in the enlisted community, but examining those correlates deserves additional study, which was beyond the scope of this project. We did note that, although the formats differ, the officer and enlisted specialty structure share the same underpinnings. This was acknowledged in 2006 when the policies for each were incorporated into the same directive, Air Force Instruction (AFI) 36-2101 (DAF, 2006).

Recommendations

Based on these conclusions, we offer the following recommendations:

- Expand the continuous process improvement initiatives under AFSO21 to include reducing the overall cycle time for classification changes.
- Revise the current classification tenets to reflect best practices from human capital management.
- Add a column to manpower requirements files for secondary specialties.
- Use the migration to DIMHRS as an opportunity to address several issues: (1) eliminate data elements that add little value or duplicate information derived elsewhere (such as qualification code 4) and (2) determine whether variants for the "any officer" codes would be useful.

- Increase rigor in the officer SEI system by establishing relationships between the SEI codes and applicable AFSCs.
- Increase the granularity of officer Intelligence specialties by using suffixes or more rigorously constructed and utilized SEIs.
- Continue research to assess the potential effects of the changing nature of work and warfare on the specialty-classification structure.

APPENDIX A

Interview Protocol

Air Force Specialty Classification Structure—Is Change Needed?

Interviewee:
Position:
Location:
Date:

Purpose: Identify changes needed in the Air Force personnel classification structure and/or documentation systems to accommodate better force development and other emerging needs.

1. Does the current classification structure and/or documentation system allow the Air Force to accurately record its manpower needs?

    - How does the system handle positions that may be filled by people from any of several specialties?
    - How does the system handle positions that require specific expertise within a specialty? (For example, the space community uses space professional experience codes [SPECs][1] to document more specific requirements.)
    - How does the system handle positions that require expertise in two specialties? (For example, acquisition and communications.)

2. Do the current classification structure and/or documentation systems hinder those people responsible for specifying the specialties reflected in manpower standards?
3. As the Air Force continues to implement various force development initiatives, do you envision any changes that may be required in the classification structure and/or documentation systems?
4. The Air Force Occupational Measurement Squadron (AFOMS) plays a very important role in the classification structure and/or documentation systems. Do the people responsible for documenting the manpower requirements provide feedback on the needs within each specialty?[2]
5. As you look to the future, do you envision any changes to the classification structure and/or documentation systems?

[1] Codes used only in the space community.

[2] This question was used to help determine whether the system was broken.

6. For this unit's function, what would it have to change/do to implement a more flexible AFSC structure? What would other units have to do to facilitate this?

   - Unit processes?
   - Other unit processes?
   - Data and documentation systems?
   - Other changes/actions needed?

7. What would be the impacts on the unit and its performance of implementing a more flexible AFSC structure? What would be the biggest challenge? Biggest benefit?

Air Force Officer Special-Experience Identifier (SEI) Codes

Table B.1
Air Force Officer Special-Experience Identifier (SEI) Codes

Activity Codes	
Code	**Title**
A	Acquisition of Systems
B	Technical Acquisition
C	Computer Systems
E	Engineering
H	Health
I	Security
L	Logistics
M	Maintenance
O	Operations
P	Personnel/Manpower Analysis
R	Research
S	Strategic Analysis
T	Tactical Analysis
W	Testing
X	Planning Programming, Budgeting
Y	Not Applicable

Experience Sets								
AA	C9	FS	KS	T0	XL	Y2	1I	4P
AE	C0	FT	KT	UA	XM	Y3	1J	4Q
AF	DE	FU	KU	UB	XN	Y4	1L	4R
AG	D2	FW	KV	UC	XO	Y5	2A	5C
AH	D3	FX	KW	UD	XQ	Y6	2B	5D
AI	EA	FZ	KX	UE	XR	Y7	2C	5E
AJ	EB	F1	KY	UF	XS	Y8	2D	5H
AK	EC	F2	LA	UG	XT	Y9	2E	5J
AM	ED	F3	LB	UH	XU	Y0	2F	6A
AN	EE	F4	LC	UI	XV	ZA	2G	6D
A5	EF	F5	LE	UJ	XW	ZB	2H	6L
BA	EG	F6	LF	UK	XX	ZC	2I	7A
BH	EH	F7	LM	UL	XY	ZD	2J	8A
BI	EI	F8	LO	UM	XZ	ZE	2K	8B
BK	EK	F9	LS	UN	X1	ZF	2L	9A
BL	EM	F0	MC	UO	X2	ZG	2M	9B
BS	EN	GA	N2	UP	X3	ZH	2N	9F
BT	EO	GB	PN	UQ	X4	ZI	2O	9G
BU	EP	JA	PO	UR	X5	ZJ	2S	9H
BW	EQ	JB	PP	US	X6	ZK	3A	9I
BX	ER	JC	PQ	UT	X7	ZL	3B	9J
B1	ES	JD	PS	UU	X8	ZM	3C	9K
B3	ET	JE	QC	UV	X9	ZN	3D	9L
B4	EU	JG	RN	UW	YA	ZO	3E	9M
B6	EV	JH	S1	UX	YB	ZP	3F	9N
B7	EW	JI	S2	UY	YC	ZQ	3G	9O
B8	EX	JJ	S3	UZ	YD	ZR	3H	9P
B9	EY	JK	S4	U1	YE	ZS	3I	9Q
B0	EZ	JL	S5	U2	YF	ZT	3J	9R
CA	E1	JM	TM	U3	YG	ZU	3K	9S
CB	E2	JN	TN	U4	YH	ZV	3L	9T
CC	E3	JO	TO	U5	YI	ZW	3M	9U
CD	E4	JP	TP	U6	YJ	ZX	3N	9V
CE	E5	JQ	TQ	U7	YK	ZY	3O	0A
CF	E6	JR	TS	U8	YL	ZZ	3P	0B
CG	FA	JS	TT	U9	YM	Z1	4A	0C
CH	FB	KA	TU	U0	YN	Z2	4B	0D
CJ	FC	KB	TV	VA	YO	Z3	4C	0E
CK	FD	KC	TW	VH	YP	Z4	4D	0F
CU	FE	KD	TX	XA	YQ	Z5	4E	0G
CY	FF	KE	TY	XB	YR	Z6	4F	0H
CZ	FG	KF	TZ	XC	YS	Z7	4G	0L
C1	FH	KG	T1	XD	YT	1A	4H	0M
C2	FI	KH	T2	XE	YU	1B	4I	0N
C3	FJ	KI	T3	XF	YV	1C	4J	0P
C4	FK	KJ	T5	XG	YW	1D	4K	0Q
C5	FL	KK	T6	XH	YX	1E	4L	0R
C6	FM	KL	T7	XI	YY	1F	4M	0S
C7	FN	KQ	T8	XJ	YZ	1G	4N	0T
C8	FO	KR	T9	XK	Y1	1H	4O	0V
								00

References

Ackerman, R. A., "New Flight Plan for Air Force Intelligence," *Signal Magazine*, 2007.

Air Force Personnel Center (AFPC), *Air Force Officer Classification Directory: The Official Guide to the Air Force Officer Classification Codes.* Randolph AFB, Texas, 2006.

Becker, G. S., *Human Capital*, Chicago, Ill.: University of Chicago Press, 1983.

Boles, B. J., *Restructured Classification System*, San Antonio, Texas, 1993.

Conley, Raymond E., Albert A. Robbert, Joseph G. Bolten, Manuel Carrillo, and Hugh G. Massey, *Maintaining the Balance Between Manpower, Skill Levels, and PERSTEMPO*, Santa Monica, Calif.: RAND Corporation, MG-492-AF, 2006. As of December 9, 2008:
http://www.rand.org/pubs/monographs/MG492

Daft, R. L., *Organization Theory and Design*, Thomson South-Western, 2007.

Defense Integrated Military Human Resources System home page, n.d. As of October 24, 2008:
http://www.dimhrs.mil

Department of Defense (DoD), *Quadrennial Defense Review Report*, Washington, D.C., February 6, 2006.

Department of the Air Force (DAF), *Designation of Air Force Enlisted Personnel as Airmen*, Air Force Regulation 39-36, Washington, D.C.: Headquarters Department of the Air Force, 1950.

———, *Warrant Officer and Airman Classification Manual*, Air Force Manual 35-1, Washington, D.C.: Headquarters Department of the Air Force, 1954.

———, *Military Personnel Classification Policy Manual (Officers, Warrant Officers, Airmen)*, Air Force Manual 35-1, Washington, D.C.: Headquarters Department of the Air Force, 1966.

———, *Determining Manpower Requirements*, Air Force Instruction 38-201,Washington, D.C.: Headquarters Department of the Air Force, 2003.

———, *Air Force Training Programming—Training Management*, Air Force Instruction 36-2201, Washington, D.C.: Headquarters Department of the Air Force, Volume 2, 2004a.

———, *Determining Non-Rated Line Officer Accession Requirements*, Washington, D.C.: Headquarters Department of the Air Force, 2004b.

———, *Assignments*, Air Force Instruction 36-2110, Washington, D.C.: Headquarters Department of the Air Force, 2005.

———, *Classifying Military Personnel (Officer and Enlisted)*, Air Force Instruction 36-2101, Washington, D.C.: Headquarters Department of the Air Force, 2006.

———, *Air Force Officer Classification Directory: The Official Guide to the Air Force Officer Classification Codes*, AFOCD, Washington, D.C.: Headquarters Air Force Personnel Center, July 31, 2007.

Department of the Army (DA), *Military Occupational Classification Structure Development and Implementation*, Army Regulation 611-1, Washington, D.C., Headquarters, Department of the Army, September 30, 1997.

———, *Commissioned Officer Development and Career Management*, Washington, D.C.: Headquarters, Department of the Army, 2005.

———, *Enlisted Assignments and Utilization*, Army Regulation 614-200, Washington, D.C.: Headquarters, Department of the Army, June 27, 2007a.

———, *Military Occupational Classification and Structure*, Army Pamphlet 611-21, Washington, D.C.: Headquarters, Department of the Army, 2007b.

Department of the Navy, *Manual of Navy Officer Manpower and Personnel Classifications*, Washington, D.C.: Headquarters, Department of the Navy, Volume 1, 2006.

Du Preez, N. D., and L. Pintelon, "The Industrial Engineer—Caught Between Two Revolutions?" *Production Planning & Control*, Vol. 8, No. 5, July 5, 1997, pp. 418–430.

Grandstaff, M. R., *Foundation of the Force: Air Force Enlisted Personnel Policy*, Washington, D.C.: Air Force History and Museums Program, 1997.

Headquarters U.S. Air Force, Office of the Deputy Chief of Staff, Personnel, *Personnel, 1 July–31 December 1951*, Washington, D.C., 1951.

Joint Chiefs of Staff (JCS), *The National Military Strategy of the United States of America*, Washington, D.C., 2004.

———, *Capstone Concept for Joint Operations*, Washington, D.C., 2005a.

———, *Department of Defense Dictionary of Military and Associated Terms*, Washington, D.C., amended August 31, 2005b.

Landry, B. J. L., Sathi Mahesh, and Sandra Hartman, "The Changing Nature of Work in the Age of e-Business," *Journal of Organizational Change Management*, Vol. 18, No.2, 2005, pp. 132–144.

Lord, W. T., *Air Force Cyber Command Strategic Vision*, Barksdale Air Force Base, La., 2007.

Markus, L. H., Helena D. Cooper-Thomas, and Keith N. Allpress, "Confounded by Competencies? An Evaluation of the Evolution and Use of Competency Models," *New Zealand Journal of Psychology*, Vol. 34, No. 2, 2005, pp. 117–126.

Mitchell, V. O., *Air Force Officers: Personnel Policy Development, 1944–1974*, Washington, D.C.: Air Force History and Museums Program, 1996.

Moore, S. C., Brent Thomas, and Raymond E. Conley, "Targeting the Occupational Skill Pairings Needed in New Air Force Colonels," Santa Monica, Calif.: RAND Corporation, 2007 (not available to the general public).

Mosher, F. C., *Democracy and the Public Service*, New York: Oxford University Press, 1982.

Robbert, A. A., Stephen M. Drezner, John E. Boon, Lawrence M. Hanser, S. Craig Moore, Lynn Scott, and Herbert J. Shukiar, *Integrated Planning for the Air force Senior Leader Workforce: Background and Methods*, Santa Monica, Calif.: RAND Corporation, TR-175-AF, 2005. As of December 9, 2008: http://www.rand.org/pubs/technical_reports/TR175/

Swanson, R. A., and E. F. Holton III, *Foundations of Human Resource Development*, San Francisco, Calif.: Berrett-Koehler Publishers, Inc., 2001.

U.S. Marine Corps (USMC), *Military Occupational Specialties Manual*, Marine Corps Order P1200.16, Washington, D.C., 2005.

Weatherly, L. A., "Human Capital—The Elusive Asset," *SHRM Research Quarterly*, 2003.